"I'm Right ... You Need to Change"

Five paths to create synergy with your life partner

By

Danyelle Beaudry-Jones with Ron Jones

authorHOUSE

1663 LIBERTY DRIVE, SUITE 200
BLOOMINGTON, INDIANA 47403
(800) 839-8640
www.authorhouse.com

This book is a work of non-fiction. Names of people and places have been changed to protect their privacy.

*© 2004 Danyelle Beaudry-Jones
All Rights Reserved.*

No part of this book may be reproduced, stored in a retrieval system, or transmitted by any means without the written permission of the author.

First published by AuthorHouse 06/23/04

ISBN: 1-4184-6817-7 (sc)

Library of Congress Control Number: 2004094099

This book is printed on acid-free paper.

*Printed in the United States of America
Bloomington, Indiana*

Acknowledgments

This book would not have been possible without my husband Ron.
We embarked on this journey together. I am forever grateful for
your willingness to share all of who you are and for
supporting me in doing the same.

A very special thanks to my parents. You gave me
your love and support in so many ways throughout my life.

Finally to my three children, Alexis, Marianne and Pascale.
You have inspired me to constantly work on myself.
I am so proud of the adults that you have become.

Preface

How to Benefit from This Book

Most of us have, at one time or another in our life, been in a committed relationship. That experience nurtured us if we felt close to our partner, if we created real intimacy and if we developed synergy together. On the other hand, if our experience was devastating and exhausting, the closeness and intimacy we desired eluded our best efforts. We generated more separation than synergy with our partner.

Ron and I guide couples through the journey of transformation from separation to synergy. We coach individuals and couples in traveling down their own specific and unique paths. We wrote this book for individuals committed to developing a nurturing and joyful relationship with their life partner.

This book is designed as an easy-to-follow guide to increase the synergy that already exists in your relationship and heal those areas that for some reason generate separation and distance.

We suggest that you read this book with your partner, but we realize that, initially, only one of you may be drawn to reading it. Share with your partner what you hold in your heart, your desires and the issues that are important to you. Be authentic about your experience. When the time is right, you can then invite your partner to share the information in this book and to participate with you in doing the transformational work described in each chapter.

Creating a successful relationship is complex and demanding. Few of us have the tools and knowledge to achieve that goal on our own. Few of us have had positive role models to guide us towards being successful in that arena of life. Our intention is to provide you with the knowledge and understanding required to meet the challenges of creating the kind of relationship you've always dreamed of having with your partner.

As you read through this book, set aside a specific time for each chapter. Working through a chapter every week or every two weeks is the ideal way to integrate the information. This will provide enough time to ponder the ideas presented and integrate them into the dynamics of your relationship. As you move from chapter to chapter, you will discover unconscious areas of your relationship, and in the process, you will discover hidden parts of yourself.

As you share your insights with your partner, you will deepen your intimacy, enrich the experience of your relationship and increase your synergy.

Table of Contents

Chapter 1
I'm Right … You Need to Change … and More 1
I'm Right … You Need to Change 1

Chapter 2
Creating Synergy or Separation 7
What Is Synergy? 7
What Is Separation? 8
Synergy Continuum 11

Chapter 3
The Five Paths for Transforming Your Relationship 13

Chapter 4
Your Minds Working Together: The Path of the Mind 17
What Is the Path of the Mind? 17
The Areas of Synergy in Your Relationship 21
Our Journey on the Path of the Mind 32

Chapter 5
Your Hearts Working Together: The Path of the Heart 43
What Is the Path of the Heart? 43
The Areas of Synergy in Your Relationship/ The Four Experiences of Emotions 66
Our Journey on the Path of the Heart 79

Chapter 6
Your Bodies Working Together: The Path of the Body 97
What Is the Path of the body? 97
The Areas of Synergy in Your Relationship 100
Our Journey on the Path of the Body 115

Chapter 7
Your Wills Working Together: The Path of the Will 123
What Is the Path of the Will?.. 123
The Areas of Synergy in Your Relationship 127
Our Journey on the Path of the Will 133

Chapter 8
Your Spirits Working Together: The Path of Spirit..........139
What Is the Path of the Spirit?.. 139
The Areas of Synergy in Your Relationship 145
Our Journey on the Path of the Spirit 166

Chapter 9
Working the Five Paths Together 175

Introduction

What Ron and I share in this book is what we have experienced in our own lives. This book is not theoretical. It is the fruit of 20 years of personal work on ourselves, with each other and with our clients. Through our commitment to doing our own personal healing work, we increased our level of intimacy, our ability to deal with day-to-day issues and our experience of joy and of love.

70 Areas of Compatibility in a Relationship

Early on in our relationship, we agreed to face each issue that showed up head on. By remaining focused on our work and keeping our commitment to resolving the issues that showed up, we discovered that there are over 70 possible areas of compatibility between partners. How you manage money, how you solve problems and how you plan your life are but a few of these opportunities for compatibility. You interact with your partner in those 70 areas. Therefore, each of these areas has the potential to either draw you closer or drive you apart from each other.

This book addresses each of these areas and shows how you can create synergy (get closer) with your partner.

The Five Dimensions of Being Human

As human beings we operate in five different dimensions.

We have a "mind" that understands and explains our experience of the world.

We have a "heart" that feels that same experience through emotions.

We have a "body" that enables us to act in the world.

We have a "will" that drives us to follow through on our commitments.

We have a spirit that connects us to our source.

Each of these dimensions is specific in its essence. For example, the mind is different from the heart. Consequently, experiencing the five dimensions requires different types of abilities and of skills. For example, in order to share your ideas in the dimension of the mind, you need to understand concepts and be able to discern facts from judgments. In order to share your emotions in the dimension of the heart, you need to be able to feel them, contain them and express them responsibly. You don't experience the mind like you would the heart or the body. The same goes for the other dimensions.

Each dimension has unique characteristics and therefore offers a unique and specific path of transformation. As human beings we relate to others in all of these five paths.

The Five Paths to Creating the Relationship You Want

Consistent with the five basic dimensions of human beings, there are five paths for creating a successful relationship with your partner. These paths are:
- the path of the "mind" - your minds working together
- the path of the "heart" - your hearts working together
- the path of the "body" - your bodies working together
- the path of the "will" - your wills working together
- the path of the "spirit" - your spirits working together.

We will walk you through each one of these paths, providing you with an understanding of the characteristics, challenges and opportunities of each one.

The 70 areas of compatibility mentioned at the beginning of this chapter are divided among the five paths. To help you understand these areas and the issues that often come up for partners, we use real-life examples taken from our coaching sessions with clients as well as from our own personal experience on a given path. In other words, we have experienced what we teach.

We Relate as We Are

Many books have been written on relationships. The unique approach presented here provides you with the tools to link the various dimensions of your relationship with the same dimensions within yourself.

This is important because the way you relate to others reflects the way you function within yourself. That is, both the strengths and limitations that you find within yourself are the same you will encounter in your relationship. For example, if you have trouble feeling your emotions, you will probably experience difficulty sharing your emotions with your partner. Similarly, if keeping your commitments is an issue in your personal life, it will most certainly impact your relationship, and so on.

All transformational work starts from within. Transforming your relationship also starts from within. As you work through each one of the paths discussed in this book, you will discover how to work on your relationship as well as how to transform yourself. When you start reviewing specific dimensions in your relationship, you will find that you are reviewing those same dimensions within yourself.

- A successful relationship can only be created by individuals who are willing to do their inner transformational work.
- A successful relationship occurs when two individuals support each other in being truly authentic, in being who they really are.
- A successful relationship is one in which two partners choose to focus on common dreams and create a deep and meaningful experience of intimacy.
- A successful relationship is one of synergy where separation is viewed as an opportunity to do one's own individual healing work.

Chapter 1

I'm Right ... You Need to Change ... and More

I'm Right ... You Need to Change

How often do you have this thought? How often do you make this statement to your partner? How often do you want to say it to your partner? "I'm right ... you need to change" must be the most recurring thought in every partner's mind.

Why is that? Being in a meaningful relationship is not easy. Here you are, two individuals with different personalities, backgrounds and experiences attempting to create an intimate and nurturing relationship. You don't fully understand each other. You don't see eye to eye. Clearly, one of you must be right. Both of you can't be right! Right?

In that case YOU must be right. After all, what you think makes so much sense. You feel strongly about your opinions. They must be the "right" opinions. If only your partner would listen. Right?

Wrong! Being righteous like this about your opinions, thoughts, beliefs or judgments is the greatest impediment to creating the relationship that you want. In fact, it is the surest way to sabotage your relationship. When you judge your partner as being "wrong" and truly believe that you are "right," you create separation. Your belief about yourself generates an equivalent belief in your partner – that he or she is right. Both of you lock into your positions and engage in a battle to the finish. Each partner holds judgments about the other's position and strives to find evidence that he or she is "right."

To create the relationship that you want, you must surrender your belief that you are right. Be prepared, letting go of that belief will raise a host of objections in your mind. All the reasons to prove that you indeed ARE right will show up. Fight back, for letting go of this belief is the essential first step toward successfully transforming your relationship.

Danyelle Beaudry-Jones with Ron Jones

Are You Ready to Change?

Take a look at your beliefs about yourself and about your partner. Do you often have the thought that you are right and your partner is wrong? Are you willing to let go of that belief and open up to different ideas and opinions, to creative solutions and new perspectives? If that is the case, you are ready to work at transforming your relationship with your partner.

Just as rigidity engenders rigidity, flexibility engenders flexibility and openness engenders openness. As a result, when you let go of your belief that you are right, you are creating the space for your partner to do the same. What a great way to start transforming your relationship together.

Four additional conditions must exist in order to transform your relationship. These four key elements will ensure that all your efforts at transforming your relationship are fruitful. Without these conditions in place, no change is possible.

Condition #1: Believe in what you want to create! Do you harbor thoughts such as, "She'll never change," "He doesn't understand me" or "What's the use of trying, nothing ever changes"? If you nurture such thoughts and believe they are true, you are sabotaging any chance that you may have at creating the relationship you want with your partner.

You need to believe that you can transform your relationship; that you can create the experience you want in your relationship. What you see in your mind, you create in your life! In every moment and with every thought you have about your relationship, you are creating your relationship. So when you project negative beliefs about your relationship into the future, you are creating your relationship in the image of those beliefs.

Let go of your negative beliefs and learn to develop positive ones. Instead of thinking "What's the use of trying, nothing ever changes," think "We haven't yet found the way, I know that we will and I'm committed to doing what it takes." Instead of thinking "She'll never change," think "We're both working on ourselves and we'll find a solution." As you work to replace negative beliefs with positive beliefs about your relationship, you will notice how joy replaces fear or sadness!!!

In the process of changing, your mind may come up with a list of reasons and facts to prove that your negative beliefs are valid. Know that things have not changed up to now because you haven't gone to the bottom of whatever issue is troubling the relationship. There is always a higher perspective on any given situation, a lesson to learn and a greater experience of love to attain. Until you have discovered the opportunity hidden behind every conflict or under every misunderstanding, the outcome will remain the same and you won't be able to realize the potential of your relationship.

Choose to create positive beliefs, let go of the negative beliefs that hold you back!

Condition #2: View your relationship as a third entity! We hold the relationship as a third entity ... sort of like having a child. Like a child, the relationship needs constant nurturing and careful monitoring to thrive. Like a child, your relationship has positive attributes that need reinforcement and negative attributes that need healing and realignment.

As adults, you are responsible for everything that happens in your relationship, for your total experience of it. Transforming your relationship will not happen without you deciding as individuals and as a couple to invest the time and the energy necessary to do your healing work.

Ironically, you invest in the maintenance of your home and of our cars, but when do you invest in your relationship? The time is now; the opportunity is in this book. Plan specific times to read the book together!

Condition #3: Leave the past behind! To create anew, you must start with a clean slate. If you haven't forgiven your partner for a specific event that happened a while back and are holding on to resentment from the past, you won't be able to transform your relationship into the nurturing and joy-filled experience you want it to be.

Resentment is a poison that infiltrates every part of your being. It leaves no place for love. Resentment comes out "sideways" as inappropriate expressions of anger, as expressions of depression or as negative beliefs about your partner. When you interact with your partner from a state of resentment, your creative energy is channeled into making your partner wrong. You find proof in day-to-day occurrences.

Move beyond this stage. Free your creative energy; let go of your resentments.

As a first step, become conscious of what you are holding on to. Then communicate those resentments to your partner and after discussing them, let them go.

What resentments do you hold on to?

Release the negative emotion!

Forgive your partner! Forgive yourself for what you held on to!

Condition #4: Let go of fear! Being in a relationship can be an experience of pure joy or it can be an experience of excruciating pain. What it is depends on where your consciousness is. As human beings, we can operate in two different levels of consciousness. We can live our life from our Ego consciousness or from our Authentic Self consciousness. How can you differentiate between these two? Ego consciousness is rooted in righteousness and in fear. You experience life as a constant struggle to prove that you are right and you make decisions and choices to avoid pain. On the other hand, Authentic Self consciousness is rooted in openness, flexibility and a deep experience of trust. You are open to opinions or solutions different from your own, and you make decisions and choices to increase your experience of love. How do you operate as partners in your relationship? Is your relationship a meeting of two Egos or is it a meeting of two Authentic Selves.

When you are in an intimate relationship, you are at your most vulnerable. Being vulnerable means that you are emotionally open. Being open can be frightening. For this reason you are often the most defensive. You may reveal parts of yourself that you are trying to hide ... even from yourself. You may reveal parts of yourself that you have hidden unconsciously for most of your life.

The Ego is that part of your self that you developed as a child in order to be able to survive. Your Ego is invested in the beliefs that it took on about you, about others and about the world. It is invested in protecting the hidden parts of your Self and in surviving as is. To do so, your Ego generates fear, specifically, fear of change.

The issues that show up in your relationship and that you never seem to be able to resolve are a direct outcome of how your Ego functions. Notice how you and your partner are afraid to open up to each other, to be vulnerable to each other, to show those parts of yourself that you don't like, to change.

Choose to let go of your position of fear. Envision that you can show all of who you are to your partner, that you are safe to be all that you can be. Envision that you have the courage to open your heart as if you were taking away the layered skin of an onion

Let go of your defensive, self-righteous position! Let go of fear! You will discover new avenues for being intimate. As you uncover who you really are, you will discover new ways to relate. In learning to function outside your Ego box, you will learn to create true synergy with your partner.

Take the time necessary to set these conditions in place. They are worth it. It's like learning to run before you learn to walk. Take the time to learn to walk. Running will then be so much easier!

- Read these conditions carefully.
- Look at yourself.
- Speak frankly and openly with your partner about the conditions.
- Choose to meet these conditions.
- Choose to be successful in transforming your relationship.

Chapter 2

Creating Synergy or Separation

A relationship is a combination of synergy and of separation. You can either create synergy or separation. You either feel close to or estranged from your partner. Being neutral is not an option. You may feel close to your partner in certain areas of your relationship at the same time as you feel estranged in other areas. For example, you may agree with your partner on how you manage money while disagreeing on how to raise your children. However, the more synergy you can create, the more successful you will be in your relationship. Let's take a closer look at how synergy and separation show up in our relationships.

What Is Synergy?

In technical terms, "synergy" is the combined action of two parts and is greater than the sum of the two. With reference to relationships, we use the term synergy to indicate that you and your partner generate more joy, love, excitement, intimacy and success "together" than you would do individually.

To get a sense of what synergy means, think back to the times when you and your partner experienced excitement together. The feelings expanded beyond your original, individual experience of them, "I was excited before, but after we talked, I was really excited." You experience greater joy and excitement with your partner when you share a common interest with the same passion. You experience greater joy and excitement with your partner when you resolve an issue and come to a consensus on an action plan. In brief, you are working together, in alignment with each other in a positive way.

Generating synergy increases your own well-being as well as of that of your relationship. Synergy generates an experience of intimacy with your partner as it increases your experience of the relationship as a safe and nurturing place to be yourself.

In the following chapters, you will learn how to increase your experience of synergy with your partner and therefore create a happier and more satisfying relationship.

What Is Separation?

In technical terms, "separation" is the act of being disconnected, apart, isolated and detached from something or someone. In reference to relationships, we use the term separation to indicate that you and your partner generate more pain, more anger and more sadness with each other and more isolation from each other.

You experience greater anger with your partner when you are pushing each other's buttons and when you are fighting. You experience greater anger with your partner when you blame each other and when you project your feelings of anger on to each other. You experience greater anger when you disagree with your partner on how to manage money. In brief, you are working together, in alignment with each other, in a negative way. You are both creating anger together.

You experience a greater sense of isolation:
- When you and your partner don't agree on a common vision or on common goals.
- When you don't understand why your partner is upset.
- When you cannot communicate your feelings or when you hold different positions on an issue.
- When you don't share activities together and lead separate lives while living in the same house.

In brief, you are working separately to achieve different goals. You have totally opposite thoughts, feelings, experiences or positions about an issue and you don't accept the other's point of view.

Separation decreases the well-being of each partner and of the relationship. It generates an experience of isolation with your partner as it decreases your experience of the relationship as a safe and nurturing place to be.

In this book you will learn how to transform separation into synergy.

Remember, you want to:
- Increase the synergy in your relationship!

I'm Right...You Need to Change

- Decrease the separation in your relationship!
- Synergy or Separation?

How do you know if you are experiencing synergy or if you are experiencing separation with your partner?

Usually, if you experience anger, sadness, frustration or fear, you are likely experiencing separation. If, on the other hand, you are experiencing love, joy, compassion and excitement, you are most likely experiencing synergy with your partner.

Another way of knowing whether or not you are in positive synergy with your partner is to use the synergy continuum. This helpful tool indicates for each of the areas to be discussed whether you are in separation or in synergy with your partner.

Take a look at the model at the end of this section. The left side of the arrow represents separation, what you don't want in your relationship. The right side represents synergy, what you want to create with your partner. Notice the four words written inside the arrow: contempt, disagree, accept/honor and agree.

The first two, "contempt" and "disagree," indicate that you hold a negative view of your partner's position on a particular issue. For example, you may have contempt for how your partner manages money or you may disagree with how your partner raises your children. These two positions on the continuum represent a state of separation that ranges from an acute experience of separation (contempt) to a milder form of separation (disagree). However, both positions increase your experience of pain, anger, sadness and isolation in your relationship.

The other two positions, "accept/honor" and "agree," indicate that you hold a positive view of your partner's position on an issue. For example, you may accept and honor your partner's political views even if they are not your own or you may agree with your partner's spiritual beliefs. These two positions on the continuum represent a state of synergy that ranges from a peaceful joyous experience (accept/honor) to an exciting and exhilarating experience (agree). Accepting/honoring and agreeing with your partner increase your experience of joy, love and compassion in your relationship.

As mentioned, there are 70 areas of compatibility between partners spread across the five paths we mentioned earlier and that are the cornerstone of this book. Each one of these areas is an opportunity to create synergy or to create separation with your partner.

In our classes and coaching sessions we find that most partners are in synergy in 80 percent or more of the areas of compatibility. Yet, they often experience their relationship as a failure. The reason is that the areas of separation "infect" the other more positive areas of the relationship. For example, it may be difficult to enjoy sexual intimacy if you have unresolved issues around raising kids or planning a vacation. That is, the unresolved issues generate resentment, and the resentment in turn blocks the way to love and to intimacy.

The first step to increasing synergy with you partner is to become aware of your respective positions for each of the areas of your relationship. Are you in agreement or in contempt with how your partner expresses anger? Do you honor/accept your partner's goals in life or do you disagree with them? You may be in synergy (honor/accept or agree) with your partner for 85 percent of the areas of your relationship. These areas will bring great comfort and joy for both of you. However, as mentioned, if you don't address the other 15 percent of the areas that are in separation (contempt or disagree), these will eventually erode the love and joy that you share together.

For this reason, it is urgent and important to identify the areas where you experience separation and to resolve the underlying issues. Without awareness of your respective positions on specific issues, there can be no improvement.

The next chapters will enable you and your partner to become aware of your respective positions on the Synergy Continuum and to discover exciting ways to increase your synergy together.

Synergy Continuum

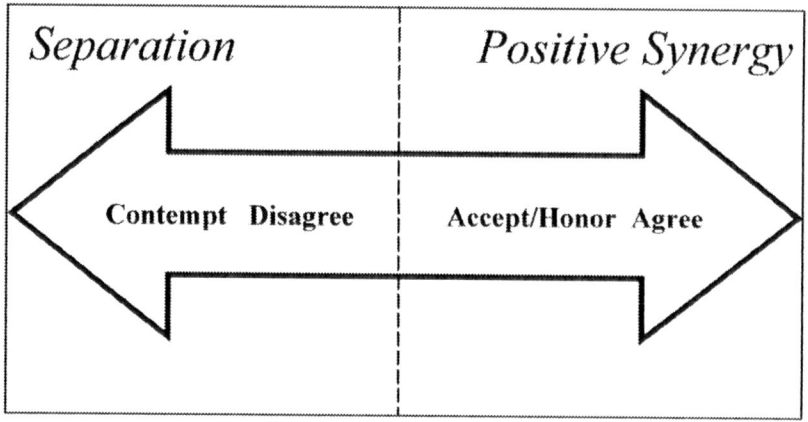

Chapter 3

The Five Paths for Transforming Your Relationship

If you want your relationship to be successful, it is not enough to share common goals with your partner. It is not enough to be able to communicate your feelings. It is not enough to be able to easily take care of your children or other ongoing responsibilities. It is not enough to share common spiritual beliefs.

Being successful in a relationship is all of the above and a lot more. Being successful in a relationship is as complex as we are as human beings. Let's start from that assumption.

As we mentioned earlier, human beings function in five different dimensions.

1. "We have a mind" with which we produce ideas, beliefs, concepts, judgments and with which we can discern facts. "We are thinking creatures."
2. "We have a heart" that feels, expresses, listens to and channels emotions such as anger, joy, excitement, fear, sadness, shame and love. "We are feeling creatures."
3. "We have a body" that enables us to interact with the world. Our body enables us to work, to exercise, to eat, to enjoy all the physical dimensions of our existence. "We are moving creatures."
4. "We have a will" that transforms thoughts into actions. Without our will, we wouldn't be able to actualize our dreams. "We are willing creatures."
5. "We have a spirit" that sources our life. We have a relationship with God. We may have differing experiences of God and give this higher being different names, but we all have an understanding and a relationship with what we consider as our source. "We are spiritual creatures."

Our relationships also operate in five dimensions.

1. We share our minds with others. We share visions, goals, ideas and beliefs. In your relationship with your life partner, "your minds work together."

2. We share our emotions with others. We express, listen to and feel anger, joy all the emotions that our heart produces. In your relationship with your life partner, "your hearts work together."
3. We share our actions with others. We do activities together, we take care of kids, we take care of our budget or of our house. In your relationship with your life partner, "your bodies work together."
4. We share our commitments with others. We want to achieve certain things and agree to commit and to follow through with others. In your relationship with your life partner, "your wills work together."
5. We share our spiritual beliefs and practices with others. We talk about God or some higher being, we pray together or meditate together. In your relationship with your life partner, "your spirits work together."

In brief, as we are, so we relate. At issue here is not whether or not we relate on those five dimensions but how we relate on them.

Do you, as partners, create positive synergy with your minds? Do you share common goals and a common vision, for example?

Do you, as partners, create positive synergy with your hearts? Are you able to feel, express responsibly and listen to your partner's emotions and channel them in creative endeavors?

Do you, as partners, create positive synergy with your bodies? Do you share housecleaning tasks, raise your kids with joy aligned to how you live your day-to-day together? Do you manage your budgets well together?

Do you, as partners, create positive synergy with your wills? Do you follow through on your commitments? Do you take time for your relationship? Do you both take leadership in making your relationship work?

Do you, as partners, create positive synergy with your spirits? Do you pray together and meditate? Do you agree on your understanding of God or some other higher being and support each other in your spiritual paths?

Each couple is different. As you think about the five dimensions, you may find that you and your partner have a high degree of synergy with your minds. That is, you may have clear goals and a common vision. At the same time, you may have a low level of synergy in your hearts. That is, you may be unable to express anger in a responsible way and choose to refrain from even trying. Another couple may experience total alignment and positive synergy in their hearts. They can express and listen to each other's emotions. However, they may have problems in dealing with day-to-day activities such as housekeeping.

Each relationship is a unique expression of the differences and similarities between partners and of the original personalities of each partner. For this reason, each couple needs to define its own plan for transforming the relationship. One thing is certain, whatever the differences between couples, all transformational work will result in traveling down one or more of the five paths.

The next five chapters will enable you and your partner to:
- better understand each of the five paths to create greater synergy
- learn how to improve the specific areas that give you difficulty within each path
- find out about other's couples' issues and success stories
- get a bird's eye view of your own level of synergy.

Have a wonderful journey traveling along these exciting transformational paths!!!

Chapter 4

Your Minds Working Together
The Path of the Mind

What Is the Path of the Mind?

Each of the five paths is a different adventure. The differences are as great as if you were traveling to different parts of the world. And the preparation, including the items you bring along, required for taking the trips is just as varied. You would not embark on an African safari with the same traveling gear as you would a trip to the North Pole. Nor would you use the same currency and language when traveling in China as you would in France. In the same way, each one of the five paths for creating synergy in your relationship has its own set of requirements for successfully completing the journey. In order to travel successfully on the path of the mind, the focus of this chapter, you will need understanding, discernment and structure.

Understanding Reality

Your mind makes sense of your experiences and formulates a set of beliefs about the world and your place in it. That is, your mind understands your experience of the environment that surrounds you as well as your inner reality so that you can survive and function successfully. As children, you struggled to make sense of your parents' reactions to situations and to events so you could understand what rules to follow and learn to survive. For example, you may have learned that your parents did not welcome you asking questions or that expressing anger was strictly forbidden. As adults, you use your mind to receive and process information and to identify which actions are the most appropriate.

Your minds create concepts, ideas and common languages so that you can understand yourself and others and so that you can relate to others. Without common concepts, ideas and languages, communication would be restricted to an experience of feelings. You would feel that someone is communicating but you would not comprehend what that communication was about. With your minds, you can understand and share what you experience.

Discernment

Discernment is the key to making informed decisions and to successfully solving problems. Your mind differentiates between different aspects of your experience. For example, a fact is different from a judgment, and a belief is different from a fact. In other words, you can train your mind to recognize objective reality and to separate it from your subjective experience.

Objective reality is measurable and quantifiable and can be verified by different individuals. It is fact based. Subjective reality, on the other hand, is your experience of a fact based on your beliefs and opinions about life and about yourself; it is your interpretation of that fact. For example, your partner is 15 minutes late for supper. That is a fact. Annoyed, you think, "My partner does not respect me." That is a judgment/thought based upon your beliefs about your partner and about yourself. Your ability to discern the objective truth from your own experience impacts the quality of your decisions. That is, if you truly believe that your partner does not respect you, you will decide on a very different course of action than if you focus on the fact that your partner is 15 minutes late. In one instance (lack of respect), you may decide to withhold your love. However, if you simply acknowledge that your partner is 15 minutes late, you may choose to drop the issue.

Structuring Your Future

In addition to helping you understand your present, your mind also enables you to structure your future. You can formulate a vision for yourself, identify goals and create a plan to achieve them. Your mind enables you to create the life that you want. What you believe in, you can create. What you see in your mind's eye, you can bring into existence. Do you have a retirement plan or are you establishing specific goals for your financial portfolio. You are using your mind to shape your future.

Synergy, Understanding and Discernment

Let us see how these attributes of the mind affect the synergy in your relationship. You can create synergy with your partner on the path of the mind when you understand reality in a way that makes sense to both of you. Being able to distinguish facts from judgments

I'm Right...You Need to Change

helps you to make sense of what is true and of what stems from your judgments and your set of beliefs. These abilities support you in making the right decisions and solving problems efficiently with your partner.

As partners, you may have different levels of mental ability, which affect your level of synergy. For example, if one partner can discern facts from judgments and the other can't, discussions will be arduous and may end in a stalemate. If you can both learn to recognize the facts of a given situation and can recognize your judgments for what they are, you can use your discussions as a springboard for making the right decisions and finding the appropriate solutions.

Synergy, Structuring the Future

Creating synergy with your partner is also about formulating a vision that you both can support, goals that you believe in and a plan that you both deem feasible. If one partner has a clear vision for his or her life and the other doesn't, you can't create a common vision. For this reason, it is important for both partners to acquire tools that help them understand reality as it is, the truth about it, and ways to shape the future, as they want it to be.

There are many opportunities to create synergy with your partner on the path of the mind. These can be found in the areas listed below.

- Values (what is important in life, such as love, money, spiritual practices etc.)
- Vision (defining where you see yourselves in 5, 10 or 15 years)
- Goals (specific things you wish to achieve, such as an income of 50,000 by 2005, total savings of 400,000 by 2010, two trips a year by 2005, be a chiropractor, etc.)
- Plan for life (specific activities you need to do to achieve your goals, such as a budget that includes percentage of income saved, studying at a chiropractic college)
- Discerning facts from judgments
- Decision making (ability to easily make decisions)
- Problem solving (ability to easily solve problems)
- Communicating about ideas and concepts

Now let us discuss each of these areas in more detail to help you see the opportunities for growth and increased synergy in your relationship.

The Areas of Synergy in Your Relationship

Sharing Common Values In Life

All partners need to discuss their life values. What is important to you? Is it your relationship, your future family or your career? Are your spiritual beliefs and practices important? Talking about values helps you understand your partner's daily priorities. If you prefer a quiet lifestyle so that you can pursue your spiritual practices and your partner prefers a busy social life, your differing life values could potentially generate conflict and separation.

Have in-depth discussions about your values. However, talking about values is not enough. Actions speak louder than words. Take a good look at your life! Ask your partner to do the same. How do you spend your time? Do you spend most of your time pursuing your career or building a family? Do you spend more time praying and meditating or watching television? Whatever you spend your time on reflects your true values.

Couples often express how much they value their relationship. However, when asked how much time they spend talking together or working through their issues, they come up with a lot of reasons why their actions don't reflect their professed values: they have a job that requires their total commitment, the children require their constant attention, and so on. For example, if you profess that your family is important to you, yet you miss out on all of your children's school performances or are always late for supper, actions indicate that your priority is obviously not your family.

If you and your partner are at odds about how you spend your time, this probably reflects different values. If you seem to have different priorities, take the time to talk about your values in life. Identify what values you really share. Make those values the center of your life together. Be honest about the time that you "really" allocate to what you say is important. Commit to reflecting in your daily schedule the real priorities that you choose together.

Having common values and developing a daily schedule that reflects those values will increase the level of synergy between you. Managing the family needs or supporting each other's career, for example, will be granted the needed attention and time. You will manage your life according to your values.

Creating a Vision, Goals and a Plan

Structuring your future is a three-part process. The first part is about establishing a "vision" for yourself and for the two of you. This involves asking questions such as: Where do you want to be in 5, 10, 20 years?

Your future vision indicates what your dreams are. Do you want to retire in Hawaii or in Florida or stay right where you are? When you do retire, what do you want to do? Do you want to travel around the country in a Winnebago or simply enjoy two or three trips a year? The dream you have for your life evolves. That is, what you want for yourself in 5 years is probably different from what you want for yourself in 20 years.

The second part of the process has to do with your "goals." Your goals are the milestones you must achieve in order to actualize your vision. Let's say that your vision is to live in Hawaii when you retire. To actualize that vision, you need to develop a series of goals. One of those goals may be to save $10,000.00 a year for 20 years so that you can afford to move to Hawaii. Another goal may be to buy a house now and rent it out as an investment until you retire. You can establish goals yearly and they can be long-term.

The third part of the process relates to your "plan for life." Your plan describes the specific activities that you need to engage in to achieve the goals you have set for your life. For example, if you have the goal of buying a house in Hawaii, you will need to do research on houses for sale in Hawaii. Whatever the goal, you will need to do whatever is needed to achieve it. That is the plan.

Take the time to share your vision with your partner. Find out how you can align your separate visions to design a shared one. Once you've taken that step and you agree on a dream, it is much easier to identify specific goals and a related plan that will enable you to make it happen.

Having a common vision, shared goals and a shared plan greatly increases day-to-day synergy. You now have a purpose for saving money. You now share excitement about a project that you are doing! All that you do together is guided by your shared alignment.

This step isn't always easy for couples. Sometimes, partners have totally different dreams. Unfortunately, they may not have discussed their dreams prior to their marriage or entering a committed relationship. If it is impossible for them to align their vision, their goals and their plan, the viability of the relationship becomes questionable. For example, it will be difficult for a marriage to survive if one partner wants to retire in Hawaii while the other wants to retire in Alaska, or if one partner wants to have children and the other doesn't.

In other cases, one partner has a lot more clarity about his or her vision, goals and plan for life than the other. It is much easier for some individuals to see themselves projected in the future than it is for others who have a more day-to-day focus. Different levels of ability and different levels of interest in visioning and in planning do not mean that synergy between partners is impossible. However, one partner may lead the process and also lead the visioning exercise. The other partner may come up with more goals and with more activities for the plan. It is important that both support and maintain the focus on the vision and that as you gradually reach your goals you participate together in the implementation the plan.

Discerning Facts from Judgments and Emotions

The ability to discern facts from judgments and emotions helps you and your partner manage and/or avoid endless discussions, disagreements, fights and bickering.

As you become proficient in using this skill, you will become an expert at discerning what is really happening (the truth/facts) and at acknowledging what are essentially your own judgments.

What is a judgment? Judgments are based on our beliefs. Typically, we take on our parents' beliefs or make them up from our experience as children. We do so without discernment. Children are like sponges; they absorb water whether that water is clear or muddied. As children, we did not know how our beliefs would serve us. Indeed, many of our beliefs do not serve us well. They limit our ability to understand reality and the experiences of others. They create separation from others because beliefs speak of our subjective reality, not of the objective truth. Having our own subjective reality is fine as long as we recognize it as such. As children, we could not separate what we experienced as our own truth. For example, if your dad was angry, you probably took it personally. You may have thought that you were to blame. As a child you didn't have the ability to discern that your father's anger was his own and not of your making. You didn't know that your father could have made a different choice. You took it on as if you were somehow responsible.

Some of our beliefs about the world are also a product of our inner child wounds. For example, if you were raised in a strict household where asking questions was viewed as a lack of respect, you may have taken on a belief that to be loved you must never question what your parents say. As an adult this will manifest itself as a belief that in order to be successful, you must obey the rules at all cost. This belief limits your ability to explore possibilities. So, when you discuss a situation with your partner and you are convinced of this belief, you will not be able to hear your partner's perspective, especially if it reflects a different, more lenient point of view.

We judge as we believe. Therefore, our judgments must be acknowledged for what they are. They are not the truth about a situation but only an interpretation of the truth.

What is a fact? A fact is a piece of information that is objective and can be seen and understood by all. In a room, everyone can see the window. However, one person may say that he perceives the window as small whereas someone else may perceive it to be of average size. If both individuals measured the window and found out that it measures 24 inches by 48 inches, their observation would now be a fact.

No one can dispute facts: no one can deny them. As we saw earlier, however, anyone can argue about a judgment.

What is an emotion? An emotion is a state of feeling. An emotion is not rational, nor can it be explained or structured. The basic canvas that we use for emotions includes anger, joy, sadness, shame, love, fear and excitement. Emotions must be acknowledged for what they are.

Putting it all together, let's illustrate how facts, judgments and emotions operate together with an example. I arrive 15 minutes late for supper. Me being late by 15 minutes is a "fact." My partner thinks, "You don't respect me when you are late." That is a "judgment." My partner is angry. The anger stems from the judgment my partner has made about the fact that I am late by 15 minutes. Someone else could have made a different judgment. They could have had no reaction, or they could have been sad and thought that I didn't love them. Judgments are our own creations. Facts exist beyond our experience of them.

Judgments are opinions based on perceptions, interpretations, belief systems and inner child wounds. We believe our judgments because they are accompanied by strong emotions. That is, how can my judgments be wrong when I feel so strongly about them?

When a statement elicits a strong reaction inside of us, chances are it is a judgment. Facts, unless they bring about real, immediate pain such as some form of abuse or the loss of a loved one, seldom provoke a strong reaction. They simply are.

Imagine your partner telling you that when you are late you don't respect him. You may have a different opinion on this issue. For you being late may have nothing to do with respecting your partner. Both of you will probably try to convince the other of the "right" judgment. You'll end up angry and frustrated.

When you and your partner learn to discern facts from judgments and from emotions, you will no longer be confused by the different experiences you are having and the different types of information you are receiving. You will be able to see the truth about a situation (the facts), acknowledge the judgments that you are both making and link those with the emotions you are feeling.

We will talk a lot more about this in the next chapter. Let us simply note at this point that the skill to discern fact, judgment and emotion opens a window of opportunity to access your inner child wounds and to do your own emotional healing. Being able to agree with your partner on what the facts are will also increase your synergy. You will understand reality in the same way. Being able to share the judgments that you each have with each other will also increase your synergy.

Making Decisions and Problem Solving Together

Decision making and problem solving are often key issues for couples wanting to improve their relationship. A couple is made up of two distinct and very different individuals with opinions and beliefs/wounds that reflect those differences. Those divergent opinions and beliefs often lead to difficulty in making decisions and solving problems. Since both partners experience life in their own unique way, they will inevitably come up with unique solutions tailored to their vision and to their understanding of life.

When a decision must be made regarding a specific issue or a family project, or when a problem requires resolution, both partners may become very emotional about what they consider to be the ideal outcome. They may not have taken the time to fully understand the situation. They may have come to a decision in their own minds based exclusively on their own judgments and emotions about the situation at hand.

There are a series of steps that couples can follow to improve their decision-making and problem-solving abilities. These are as follows.

Step 1: What is your intention? The first step in any decision-making or problem-solving process for couples is to notice what their intention is. Do you know that you have the right decision or solution for the problem? Do you want to convince your partner that your decision or solution is the "right" one? Or are you more interested in reaching an outcome that will increase your level of synergy together?

The intention with which you enter any decision-making or problem-solving process will determine not only the outcome you will reach but also the process you follow. If, for example, you have already decided that you want to go to Europe for your holiday and you want to convince your partner of the validity of that decision, you will think of all the possible reasons for going there and demonstrate no openness to hearing your partner's point of view. Your mind is already made up.

However, if you want to find a vacation spot that both you and your partner will agree on, you will be open to listening to your partner's ideas and you will want to find a solution that creates more synergy. Before you attempt to make a decision or solve a problem, check your intention. Ask your partner to do the same. Don't proceed to the next step unless your intention is to create synergy with your partner and you are willing to let go of your predetermined decision or solution.

Step 2: What are the facts, the judgments and the emotions? Before you start considering the different options for a given decision or solution, clarify with your partner what the facts are in the situation you are focused on. If you want to make a decision around your next vacation, what budget do you have? What other facts are related to this situation? Do you have children? Are you planning on taking them along or will you have to find babysitters? Also notice what your respective judgments are about taking a vacation. Are you excited about it? Now is the time to practice your skill at discerning facts from judgments and from emotions.

Once you have clearly identified the facts, the judgments and the emotions, take the time to communicate about them. Find a common set of facts that both of you can agree on. You will be able to use these in the next step of your process. You are now ready to make a decision or to find a solution that will work for both of you.

Step 3: What are your needs and wants? As mentioned earlier, your relationship is a third entity. As such, it has specific needs and/or wants that may be different from the individual needs and wants of each partner. For instance, you and your partner have had a busy week. You haven't had time to connect with each other except the casual, "Hi, how was your day!" A lot of things have been left unsaid and you experience separation with your partner. You feel distant. Your heart is not as open as it usually is. You are tired. All you want to do is curl up in bed and read. Your partner, on the other hand, wants to watch television.

The relationship as a third entity requires that both of you spend some time together and share those unexpressed thoughts and feelings. In this instance, you and your partner have totally different needs and wants than those of the relationship. What choices will you make? When the needs of the relationship are unmet, the relationship suffers. No wonder you don't have a deeper experience of intimacy with your partner! The same principle applies to decision making and problem solving. When you want to make a decision or you want to solve a problem, identify not only your needs and wants as well as those of your partner, but also those of the relationship.

To find out about your relationship's needs and wants, revisit your vision for your relationship. Remember what kind of relationship you want. If you want a relationship that thrives, what has to happen? You will need time and specific activities to create intimacy and to achieve the vision that you hold for your relationship. You may want to go for walks together on a regular basis, enjoy a meal out once a week or give each other massages every two weeks.

Feeling love for your partner is not enough. This feeling has to be regenerated continuously through specific activities. Spending time together, having fun together, sharing your deepest thoughts and feelings with each other may be some of the activities you choose to integrate in your schedule.

If a decision or a problem includes other members of the family, also consider their needs and wants. Whoever is involved in the decision you are making or in the problem you are solving should be part of the process.

Step 4: Making a decision, finding a solution Now think of a few decisions or solutions that you can adopt. Once you have written them down, check them against the list of facts identified under Step 2 and the lists of needs and of wants developed in Step 3. Choose the decision or solution that fits those lists. Rework your decision and/or your solution until you have found one that meets all your needs and wants and that takes into account all the facts.

Making a decision or solving a problem with your partner in a harmonious and aligned manner is exciting. You both know that your individual needs were taken into account, so there is no resentment with the decision or the solution chosen. You feel closer to your partner. You become total partners in implementing the decision or the solution. What a great way to increase your synergy!

Communicating about Ideas and Concepts

Sharing your ideas with your partner may be easy for you or it may be difficult.

Each couple has to develop their own unique language. This takes a great deal of work and perseverance as there may be roadblocks along the way. Here are some of the roadblocks that you may encounter on the journey to developing your own special language. As you will note, most difficulties stem from differences in background – the kind of communication style you grew up with.

You and your partner are from different backgrounds. As children, you learned to use language in different ways. You may have read a lot more than your partner and therefore you now have a larger vocabulary. You have more vocabulary available to you. You may have been reprimanded as a child for your direct way of saying things. Perhaps you learned to ask questions and to never say openly what you really think. Your partner, on the other hand, was always rewarded for being honest and straightforward.

Keeping these differences in mind, see what happens when you are attempting to have a conversation. You use words your partner is not familiar with. Your partner is uncomfortable and judges himself as being less intelligent than you. You avoid saying what you feel and what you think, asking questions in the hope that your partner will guess what you want to say. Your partner, on the other hand, wants to know what you really think. He is frustrated and judges you for being evasive and dishonest. You feel guilty for not being able to speak clearly about what you really think.

Sound familiar? Unless you have spent time talking about your differences and acknowledging how you used language as a child, all of this is unconscious. What you may be clear about is that communicating with your partner is no easy task.

Due to our different backgrounds, sometimes we learned different meanings for the same words. We were exposed as children to a greater or a lesser number of words. We learned a way to communicate. We learned how to be direct or evasive. We learned that it was okay to ask questions or that it was not. Most of our communication skills were handed down to us by our family of origin and by our immediate group of friends. Our schooling also trained us in the art of using words and communicating skills.

If you are having trouble communicating with your partner, find out what the problem really is. What are the facts behind your problems with communication? Is it the meaning that you give to words? Men sometimes use words with a precise meaning, whereas women use words to convey an emotion. Is that the case? Is it your communication style that is different? Find out what the source of the problem is and then gradually come up with your own language.

Spend time agreeing on the meaning of words. It's worth it. This is not about convincing your partner to adopt your definition of a word or of an expression. This is about identifying a common definition that you can both relate to.

Spend time noticing your different styles. What are the strengths and weaknesses of each style? When is it preferable to be direct? When is it advisable to simply ask questions? Agree on how you want to communicate together. Establish your own guidelines for effective communication.

By taking the time to understand the meaning of words and to discover your different styles, you are investing in the future. The language you are building together will enable you to create greater intimacy. And with greater intimacy comes greater synergy.

YOUR SYNERGY CHECKLIST

REMEMBER:

You can increase your synergy on the path of the mind if you:
- Share common values (you value the same things in life)
- Share a common vision for your relationship (you share the same dreams about your life in 5, 10, and 15 years)
- Share common goals for your relationship (you pursue goals together as a couple)
- Share a plan for your relationship (you agree on what activities you have to do to achieve the goals for your couple)
- Support each other's individual vision, goals and plan for life
- Align your relationship's vision, goals and plan with your individual visions, goals and plans
- Learn to discern facts from judgments and use that ability to make better decisions and solve problems
- Practice efficient decision making

- Practice problem solving together
- Communicate clearly (ideas and concepts that reflect your understanding of the world: develop your own language) and effectively

How's your synergy doing?

In the next section, we discuss how Ron and I tackled our issues on the path of the mind.

Danyelle Beaudry-Jones with Ron Jones

Our Journey on the Path of the Mind

For Ron and I, the journey on the path of the mind was our most challenging of the five. The roadblocks we encountered seemed insurmountable at the beginning of our relationship. We even seriously considered going our separate ways for a while. When we first decided to have a relationship together, we made the commitment to remain partners unless our spiritual mission in life guided us on different paths. Breaking up because of disagreements or from a place of anger was not an option. We would leave each other from a place of love or we would stay and work things through. As we ventured down the path of the mind, this commitment saved our relationship.

The table that follows illustrates, for each area of the mind, our initial level of synergy and how that level evolved after we did our individual work and our work as a couple. We use the Synergy Continuum presented in Chapter 2 to indicate our synergy levels. As we mentioned, when we either "accept/honor" or "agree" with our partner's position, we create synergy. Of these two, agreement creates the greater synergy. By contrast, when we "disagree with" or are "in contempt for" each other's position, we create separation in the relationship. Of these two, being in contempt obviously creates the greater separation.

You will notice that we had quite a few areas on the path of the mind where we created separation initially. Moving from separation to synergy was not only necessary for our relationship's survival, it became a wonderful adventure in self-healing. As you read about our journey notice that the most difficult issues we encountered resulted from deep childhood wounds. We discuss each one of the areas of the path of the mind in the following pages.

Areas of the Mind	Synergy Level at the Beginning of Our Relationship	Synergy Level After We Did Our Healing Work
Shared Values	In agreement	In agreement
Common vision	In disagreement	In agreement
Common goals	In disagreement	In agreement
Common plan	In contempt	In agreement
Decision making	In disagreement	In agreement
Problem solving	In agreement	In agreement
Discern facts from judgments	In agreement	In agreement

Our Values Together

Ron and I shared common values at the onset of our relationship. We had done a lot of work in identifying what was important for each one of us in a relationship. This was not our first marriage. We knew from past experience the importance of having common values with one's partner.

Ron and I met on the Internet. As part of that process, we had written a clear description of what we wanted in a partner. At the top of the list was the importance of doing our spiritual work. Since spirituality was a passion for both of us, we made it our first selection criterion in finding a partner for life. We also discovered that we shared a number of other values. Honesty, sharing truth at all times and loyalty to friends were but a few of them. All in all, we shared most of the same values.

I had three children, Ron had none. For me family was of great importance. And Ron was willing to support me in creating an important place in our life for my family. We agreed at the very beginning to make that a priority for our relationship. To this day, two or three times a year we visit with my family in Montreal.

Sharing common values has been a great source of synergy for us. We are both quiet and introspective individuals; our passion is with our spiritual quest and with our relationship with others. We can spend hours talking about our individual work, our couple's work and our work with other people. How we use our time on a day-to-day basis testifies to our real core values. We spend our time on what is important to us, and we share what is important!!!

Our Vision, Goals and Plan

Having a vision, goals and a plan is part of the same process - that of creating a future. Creating a future together quickly became the major roadblock of our relationship.

When we met, Ron had a very successful life. He was a golf professional enjoying his semi-retirement in Sedona, Arizona. He had led a fascinating life, experimenting with different types of occupations and meeting interesting and diverse people. He had also traveled extensively. However, he had never created a vision, goals or a plan for himself. He believed that life should be lived on a day-to-day basis and that the universe or God would always take care of him.

When we met, I owned a management-consulting firm in Montreal and was a staunch believer in the need to create a vision, goals and a plan for your life. This belief was partly based on having observed the negative consequences for organizations and for individuals of not having a clear vision, goals and plan for the future. They seemed to drift from one opportunity to another. I also held the belief that each one of us is given the ability to create what we want in life. I believed that our thoughts and emotions about our future created that future. I also believed that, as human beings, it was our responsibility to use all our talents, including our ability to create. And I wanted to create a vision, goals and a plan with Ron.

"I'm right, you need to change." Given the above scenario, it should come as no surprise that we butted heads. I remember joking about the fact that we had two sets of horns, Ron is an Aries and I'm a Taurus. We certainly got our horns tangled up. When I came to the realization that Ron wanted no part of a vision, goals and a plan with me, I immediately sat in judgment of him: I was angry and sad. The compassionate, loving man whom I loved became a weak, undisciplined and immature man, or so I thought. I despised what I judged to be his lack of courage in working through creating a future together.

Before I moved to Sedona to live with Ron, we had communicated extensively about what we both wanted. I had shared my vision with him. I wanted a partner with whom I would start a business doing transformational work. I wanted to lead workshops, classes and coaching in partnership. He had supported that vision in his emails, or so I thought. He had even expressed his own interest in being involved.

When we started to live together, he refused to commit to creating that vision with me. I could never get a definite answer from him. For two years, he stayed in limbo. He couldn't choose between his life as a golf professional and starting the business with me. I was desperate and discouraged; I felt deep sadness and a lot of anger. Ron's judgments about me were that I couldn't surrender to life and live in the present moment and that I was controlling. He reacted strongly to writing a plan, viewing a plan as being constrictive. In defense of his position, he protested that there were no guarantees that he could do everything included in a plan. I tried to explain that a plan is merely a guide and that you don't have to do every single thing in the plan. A plan should be flexible and help align our actions with our vision. Ron saw it as a limitation on his ability to seize the moment and follow new opportunities that life would offer.

Our discussions around drafting a plan were the most intense of all our discussions. We disagreed on a vision and on goals. We experienced contempt for each other on whether or not to devise a plan. We were stuck and locked into a contest of trying to prove that we were right and that the other had to change. In hindsight, I can see that our individual motivation during these numerous discussions was to prove our position and to change the other. It never worked.

"Heal thyself!" Because both of us had done extensive inner healing work, we knew that our reactions to the other came from within. Why did I have contempt for Ron's position? Why did he have contempt for my position? My mind told me that he had every right to live life as he wanted. I had the same right. Yet, we both experienced very strong emotions that contradicted what our minds said.

Not wanting to give up, we started going inside to look at what triggered those reactions. I started connecting the deep feeling of sadness that I felt when Ron showed no interest in sharing my vision with identical feelings I experienced as a child. I remembered my desire as a child to share my dreams, my thoughts, my desires with my dad. I wanted to show him what I had in my heart. He never responded and never showed any interest in what was important to me. For example, he never attended any of my piano concerts.

At this point in my relationship with Ron, I re-experienced the sadness that I felt at that time. I revisited time and time again those movements of the heart towards my father. I saw myself going into the den where he watched television, trying to get his attention, wanting to share my thoughts. Time and time again I was rebuffed. The little girl inside of me was broken-hearted; I was now reliving that experience with Ron, including surrendering to the anger that I felt for my father for not showing interest in who I was and in what was important to me. Only this time, the anger was directed toward Ron.

As I allowed myself to heal those deep wounds by re-experiencing the emotional pain, I started seeing Ron's position in a different light. I became peaceful and centered. I acknowledged that he had every right to live life the way he wanted to. I started relating to his reality from the adult in me and not from my wounded child. In other words, my heart started to align with the wisdom of my mind.

Ron went through his own healing process. He looked at the contempt he felt for me and revisited the anger he was projecting on me. He discovered that he experienced a great deal of fear when he considered developing a vision, goals and a plan. Where did that fear come from? By going within and taking responsibility for his experience of me, he discovered that his fear was linked to a belief that he "wasn't good enough," that he "could never do anything right." With these beliefs active inside of him, there was no way he could hold possible the attainment of a vision, goals and a plan.

Where did these beliefs come from? He uncovered inside of him a wounded little boy who had heard time and time again that what he did wasn't good enough. Ron remembered several incidents during which his father told him that he wasn't doing it right. He also remembered how much he needed his father's love and approval and how disappointed and sad he was every time he didn't get it. Ultimately, believing that his dad thought so, he made the decision as a little boy that he wasn't good enough.

It took us almost two years to do this inner healing work with our core wounds. During that time, we stopped projecting our anger and our sadness on each other. We supported each other in feeling our wounds and in remembering those painful memories. We held each other as we allowed the sadness and the anger to flow through our bodies and to be released from our bodies.

As we became witness to each other's wounds, we opened our hearts and developed compassion not only for the other but for ourselves as well.

"Creating synergy!" This is all so clear in hindsight. The timing and duration of each transformational step is in such synchronicity. When I had almost completed my healing, so had Ron. As mentioned earlier, after experiencing my inner wounded child, I came to a place of peace and clarity. I realized that the vision that I held for my life was real and that I needed to pursue it. I was at peace with the fact that Ron might not choose that vision for himself. I was ready to move on. I communicated with him my vision about wanting someone to share doing transformational work with. I told him that I wanted to do that with him but that I was at peace with the fact that he might not make that choice. I asked him to give me a clear answer.

Having completed most of his healing, Ron was now able to make a decision. Coincidentally, rummaging through his papers one day, he discovered a text that he had written years ago. On those sheets he had recorded his desire to find a partner with whom he could do workshops and lead classes. He had forgotten about those intentions. Because of the healing work he had done, he knew that what kept him from creating a vision for himself was his fear of failure, his fear of proving to himself that he really wasn't good enough, his fear that his father was right all along.

Having confronted that fear, his heart revealed its true vision. He shared the same vision that I held in my heart. We had moved from a deep and painful separation to an exciting and nurturing state of synergy. We were ready for the next phase of our life together.

Decision Making Together

Making decisions together initially wasn't easy for us. Well, that's not quite true. We could make decisions together, or so I thought. But somewhere down the line, Ron would resent the decision, telling me that in making the decision he had given up on what he really wanted. I was flabbergasted. I had deliberately tried to make sure every time we made a decision that he totally agreed with it. I thought maybe I got too excited and didn't give him the time to consider his decision. I was taking care of him and questioning my own intentions.

We finally came to the realization that there was nothing wrong with our decision-making process. Nevertheless, Ron still felt resentment about the decisions we made. To try to find out why, he started looking within. Underneath his resentment was the fact that he gave up on what he really wanted. He said yes, agreed in words, but deep down he was making the decision to please me or so he thought.

In trying to come to grips with this dilemma, we talked at length of situations where the decision Ron had made wasn't even one that I was particularly interested in. He would try to foresee my needs and then come to a decision without asking me what I truly wanted. Often, I didn't even want what he had decided. Underneath it all was Ron's belief that he wasn't good enough. He also believed that he didn't deserve to get what he wanted in life. He didn't have the will to ask and to fight for what he wanted, so he gave up.

His was not the only healing. Ron's resentment at not getting what he wanted activated my shame. I started blaming myself for his lack of clarity, for his lack of determination. Somehow, I was responsible for not giving him the space to be clear and determined. Since early childhood, I held a belief that I was inherently bad. As a result, shame had been a big wound in my life.

When an issue arises for a couple that leads to separation, both partners usually have something to heal. If Ron was not getting what he wanted and I was inherently bad, I reasoned that I must have done something wrong. I must be too controlling: I must have overpowered him. I had to revisit that wound. I used my skill at discerning fact from judgment to ascertain what the truth was. As a result of that process, it became clear that Ron had had the opportunity to state his perspective around the decision we made. He simply did not use his prerogative to do so. Consequently, I was not responsible for that choice.

The shame that I felt was unrelated to the facts of the situation. It was generated from within. As a child, I was strong-willed and always wanted to understand why I was being asked to do certain things. When it didn't make sense to me, I would rebel. As a result, I was often told that I was difficult and insensitive. I understood that to mean that I was "bad." Healing my shame has been a constant struggle in my life. Working through Ron's resentment around the decisions that we made became a wonderful opportunity for me to heal another layer of it.

We can now easily make decisions. Ron expresses his opinions more clearly and checks inside of himself for his true position when we do make a decision. Our decision making now generates synergy. This increases our excitement and joy about the actions we take together and about the outcome we reach.

Problem Solving

Problem solving has never been much of an issue between us. Our skill at discerning fact from judgments and our ability to contain our emotions have been very helpful here. We always verify our level of comfort with the solution we've chosen and we check whether there are any leftover emotions resulting from the problem. We're good at our commitment of keeping our slate clean, our hearts open.

Discerning Fact from Judgment and Emotion

Before we got together, Ron and I had developed the skills to discern facts from judgments and from emotion. Because of all the work I had done in the emotional dimension, I could easily identify my emotions. I had learned to feel and express almost all of my emotions and I was comfortable in letting my partner be witness to them. My background as a management consultant specializing in Total Quality Management had provided me with numerous opportunities to practice discerning facts from judgments. Ron had also done extensive work in feeling his emotions and he could easily discern them from facts. In addition, the numerous workshops and classes that he had attended had also enabled him to discern facts from judgments.

We use our skills at discerning facts from judgment and emotions daily with our clients and in our own relationship. We have a flip chart constantly available for our own needs. We use it to work through identifying facts from judgments and emotions for specific issues. When one arises and our emotional charge is high, we take that time to discern. Our commitment is to nurture our relationship. Projecting anger on to each other is not nurturing, so, we refuse to do so. We know from experience that agreeing on a common set of facts creates synergy. We also know that simply sharing, accepting and honoring each other's judgments without trying to change them increases our synergy. We consciously choose to practice both of these skills.

Communicating about Ideas and Concepts

From the very beginning, communicating ideas and concepts has been a source of enjoyment for both of us. We enjoy sharing our experiences of events and people. We relish in discovering new ideas and concepts together and in linking them to knowledge that we already share. We enjoy each other's sense of humor. We have a common language that stems from our common interests.

Even though we have experienced a high level of agreement in this area, we still encountered some minor roadblocks as we learned to communicate together. As mentioned earlier in this chapter, each couple needs to develop their own language. As part of that process we came upon three roadblocks.

The first is related to the fact that my first language is French. While there are quite a few words that are identical in both languages, I sometimes used an English word with the French meaning. This caused a great deal of confusion at the beginning. We would start disagreeing on a specific sentence. Unbeknownst to both of us, we were using the same word but with different meanings. When we discovered that, we started checking the meaning of key words every time we appeared to be in disagreement. This allowed us to eliminate quickly and effectively potential sources of discord.

A second roadblock resulted from our different communication styles. Our styles are very much related to the wounds that we incurred in our childhood. For example, I am a very direct and forthright person. If I think something, intuit a feeling, have an opinion, I will express it very easily and usually with a great deal of intensity. This is tied in with my wound of not being listened to as a child. That is, I learned to speak whether others wanted to hear what I had to say or not. Ron, on the other hand, is more interested in asking questions. Instead of saying clearly what he wants, he asks questions to find out what the other wants. This is tied in with his wound of not being good enough, and therefore of thinking he has nothing interesting to say.

Initially, Ron had trouble with my style. He judged me to be too forthright and too full of myself. We have come to acknowledge the strength of each other's style. We have actually taken on each other's style. A few years ago, we attended a conference in Chicago. Ron confronted the presenters with what he believed were inaccurate statements whereas I asked a lot of questions. We laughed at how we had taken on each other's style. What a change that was!

The third roadblock has to do with how we both use words. Ron likes to be precise in the use of words. I like to paraphrase. I am often more interested in the emotion or the experience I am communicating than in the exact meaning of the word. This created some minor conflicts but we have grown to recognize our differences and to give each other leeway in choosing our preferred modes of expression.

The next chapter deals with the journey on the path of the heart. It is very different from that of the mind. And as you will notice, our experience as a couple was also very different.

Chapter 5

Your Hearts Working Together
The Path of the Heart

What Is the Path of the Heart?

As mentioned in the previous chapter, each path has its own set of navigational requirements. You cannot go down the path of the heart with the same traveling gear you used for the path of the mind. To travel successfully on the path of the heart, you need to surrender to emotions, contain emotions and tag emotions to their rightful source.

The heart feels both the inner world and the outer world and expresses that experience with emotions in the same way that the mind expresses its experience using ideas, thoughts, judgments and beliefs. We cannot have a complete experience of life only with ideas, thoughts and judgments. We need emotions to "feel" the experience we are having. The mind organizes and structures our experience; the heart feels our experience.

Our Mind Often Acts as a Barrier Between Our Consciousness and Our Emotions

Most of us try to feel our emotions with our heads. You may try to explain your emotions. "I feel angry because of the world crisis" or "I am happy because I won the lottery." As you go about finding an explanation, you avoid feeling the emotion. Every time you think about your emotion, you are avoiding feeling it. Focusing on the reason for the emotion or on the trigger for it robs you of the experience of that emotion.

Instead of being conscious of our emotions, we stay in our mind and attempt to explain or to justify how we feel. Most of our clients have a great deal of difficulty acknowledging their emotions. When we ask them what they feel, they often reply, "I feel like this is not going to work," "I feel like she is not listening to me" or "I feel like I can never say anything right." They may also respond saying, "I feel that I don't have a chance" or "I feel that my partner is not open to listening to me."

Rather than true feelings, the opening statements "I feel like" or "I feel that" usually introduce a judgment. It can be a judgment about a specific situation, about another person or about ourselves. It may even be a judgment about our emotions. "I feel like" and "I feel that " seldom introduces the expression of emotions. When you use those phrases, you are putting your mind in charge of your experience. You are bringing your consciousness into your mind instead of into your heart. To be in your heart, you need to surrender to your emotions.

Notice how often you use the expressions "I feel like" and "I feel that." To the question "What do you feel?," reply, "I feel anger or joy or sadness." In other words, reply with the emotion you are feeling right now and notice what you experience.

Surrendering to Your Emotions

When you share your emotions, do you experience a loss of control, do you experience being vulnerable? If you do, this is because the act of feeling emotions includes a form of loss of control. Emotions cannot be organized, explained or structured. Emotions must be experienced. They simply are. Emotions are energy that shows up without you ever deciding for them to do so. To illustrate, we like to use the following analogy.

Imagine that your emotions are like water in a lake. Some people go on the lake in a boat or on water skis. Others dive into the lake. When you stay in the boat or on water skis, you don't experience the water. Sitting in a boat, you watch the water and make a judgment about it. You express an idea of the lake in the form of a judgment; you do not experience the water as such. This is in essence what we do when we say "I feel like" or when we explain an emotion. We don't "feel" the emotion, we "watch" it from our mind like watching the water while sitting in a boat.

When you dive into the lake and feel the water around your body, you surrender to the feeling of the water. You become one with the water. This is what surrendering to your emotions means. You become one with your emotion in the same way that you become one with the water when you dive into the lake.

When you surrender to your emotions, you choose to feel them completely. You don't have an agenda. You don't say, "Well, I'll feel my anger for the next hour and then I'll move on to something else." When you surrender to your emotions, you allow them to run their course. For example, if you choose to feel the anger that is showing up in your body, you allow it to move in your body, you bring your consciousness into it and go for the ride.

Fear of Feeling

Most of us experience a lot of fear at the idea of surrendering to emotions. The reason is simple. As children, you couldn't cope with the intensity of some of the emotions you were feeling or were subjected to. Feeling shame, for example, would have been a devastating experience if you had not had a way of protecting yourself from it. Maybe your dad's anger was so terrifying that you learned to detach from it. You learned to understand, to explain and to hold your emotions at a distance. That distance created emotional detachment. Thus, your mind enabled you to detach yourself from your emotional experience.

To feel an emotion you need to surrender to the experience of that emotion. Surrendering to your emotions is about surrendering to the feeling of your emotions, not to the expression of it. Surrendering is not acting out your emotions. Surrendering to your emotions means that you choose to feel your emotions within, whatever they may be, with no judgment, with no restraint. Depending on the situation, you may choose not to express them to others. For example, I can surrender to feeling my anger without acting out my anger. I may experience the anger in my body without screaming it to my partner. The ability to surrender to the emotion inside of you while at the same time managing its expression indicates a high level of maturity in consciousness, awareness and discernment. That maturity comes from the fact that you choose to "own" your emotions. You are not a "victim" of your emotions and you don't want to make others responsible for having them. When you surrender to your emotions, you surrender to the inner experience of them in your body, not to the outer expression of them.

Some of us believe that feelings are dangerous. Had your parents been able to teach you that it was okay to feel, you wouldn't have taken on the belief that feelings are dangerous. Feelings are not dangerous, but we have a belief that they are. And we have a belief that we need to control them. Often, clients talk about their fear of their own anger. "If I feel my anger, I am afraid that I'll destroy everything around me" is the most common expression of that fear. In fact, the fear is related to how anger is expressed, "I'll destroy everything," more than to the actual experience of feeling anger.

As children we learned to fear emotions; our own and other people's emotions.

Your parents may have told you that "Boys don't cry" or "It's not nice to be angry". You took on your parents' beliefs about emotions. You may also have been at the receiving end of inappropriate expressions of emotions such as anger. If one or both of your parents expressed anger through verbal or physical abuse, you learned that anger hurts. Not surprisingly, you became afraid of your own anger and decided to never feel it again.

Diverting Emotions

You may also have been diverted from feeling your pain. Parents often believe that by consoling their children, they help them "feel better." Comments such as "Here, here, don't cry. Come and see mommy, she'll take away the pain" are commonplace. Your parents were probably unable to feel/stand their own painful emotions such as sadness, fear or anger, so they tried to stop you from feeling your own. These well-intentioned efforts, in reality, robbed you of your experience of feeling emotions.

You may also have been shamed for feeling and expressing your emotions. Your parents may have curbed your expression of excitement or joy. You may have heard, "Now, don't get too excited!" "Will you calm down!" "Don't get hysterical!" or "It's no reason to feel angry!" Through these words, you were shamed about your emotions.

So not only do most of us believe that feeling emotions such as anger and excitement is dangerous and fearful, we are also quite confused between feeling and expressing emotions. We'll talk more about that later.

Another reason why most of us are so uncomfortable with surrendering to our emotions is that our educational system strives to train our minds in understanding and in organizing reality.

Unfortunately, little or no attention is given to training children to surrender to, contain and tag emotions to the right source.

Containing Emotions

The ability to surrender to your emotions works in tandem with the ability to contain your emotions. When you contain your emotions, you are the container for your emotions. How do you do that? You contain your emotion, when you totally own the experience that you are having. You do not judge or blame another person for what you are feeling. You are feeling it. Think of it like filling up a balloon with water. The balloon will only be able to hold the water if it has no holes. If there is a hole, no matter how small, drops of water will leak out and, eventually, the balloon will be empty of water. It is the same with your emotions. If even a small part of you believes that others are responsible for your experience of the emotion you are feeling, you are not containing the emotion. You are giving it away.

Let's look at an example.

Your partner talks about a trip he wants to make. You experience fear inside of you. At that moment you have a choice. You may decide that your fear is related to the trip your partner wants to make; you believe that the trip is dangerous or you may decide that your fear is of your own making. Look at the facts. Is the trip really dangerous or are you imagining possible threats?

What you choose to do at that moment will directly impact your behavior. In the first case, you may believe that your fear is real and that your partner's trip is dangerous. As a result, you will try to convince your partner to cancel his trip. On the other hand, you may recognize that there are no real threats related to the trip and choose to contain the fear within yourself.

You choose to go within to investigate the real trigger for your fear. For example, you may have abandonment issues. As a child you never felt safe with your parents' love, fearful that they would abandon you. In fact, they abandoned you on an emotional level. In the current example, when your partner mentions going on a trip, that triggers the abandonment wound and fear shows up. Only if you attribute the experience of that emotion to yourself can you contain it and discover the healing opportunity encased in it.

You could have projected the fear on your partner, making him/her responsible for your experience. Yet, you chose to contain it. You looked at the facts and recognized the truth: There were no real dangers. If you throw your emotion at someone else as in screaming or shouting, you are not containing your emotion within yourself; you are giving someone else power over your experience. You are seeing them as the source of your emotion, in this instance of your anger. As a result, you become emotionally powerless. That is, if someone else is responsible for what you feel, you depend on them for your emotional experience. You cannot own something that you give away. You cannot transform something over which you have no power.

As a child, not feeling certain negative emotions was a normal defense mechanism. You were unable to contain the devastating experience of some of those negative emotions, so you denied their existence. As an adult, you no longer need that defense mechanism. You have the potential ability to contain the emotion that you are feeling. It is up to you to actualize that ability by choosing to contain your emotional experience.

Tagging Emotions

As you learn to contain the emotion you are feeling, you can learn to tag it to its rightful source. Is the emotion related to the present moment or is it resurfacing from a past experience/wound? Or is it projected onto you by someone else?

Emotions are "infectious." Have you noticed how being in the presence of someone who is positive and cheerful makes it easier for you to feel the same way? Have you also noticed how the opposite is true as well? Sometimes we hear of widows or widowers who change dramatically after the death of their spouse. All of a sudden, they are cheerful and easy to get along with, whereas in the past they may have appeared depressed or taciturn. They may have been infected by their partner's depression. This is where projection of feelings comes in.

If you feel an emotion, that is your experience. However, the emotion may not have originated with you. It may have come from someone else or even from something else. Notice how music affects your mood. Notice how reading stories of murder in your

I'm Right...You Need to Change

local newspapers affects your mood. We are all subject to emotional infections. Of course, the emotion that you feel may also be your own creation. As we saw earlier, it may be a reaction in the present moment to an immediate situation or it may be an emotion related to the re-awakening of an old wound. Being able to tag the emotion to its rightful source empowers you to choose the appropriate behavior for the situation at hand.

Let's describe a few situations to clarify the importance of tagging an emotion to its rightful source.

Situation #1: Your partner believes that your children must be punished every time they break a family rule. Your partner is not angry but is simply stating a point of view that is different from yours. When you state your own position, your partner comes back with another argument that supports his or her position. "You feel tremendous anger inside of you and you notice that you want to scream at your partner."

Situation #2: You are having a disagreement with your partner about your plans for the summer vacation. All of a sudden, your partner starts screaming at you and accuses you of being selfish. "You feel your partner's anger in your body."

Situation #3: You and your partner are having an argument about the budget. As the discussion becomes more and more intense, your partner is so frustrated that he hits you on the arm. "You notice that anger shows up in your body."

How to you know what the source of the anger is? We discussed at length in Chapter 4 the skill of discerning between fact, judgment and emotions. This is one instance where that skill is especially useful. If you feel an emotion and you have surrendered to it and contained it, look at the facts of the situation. What was said or done?

Then look at your judgment. Is your emotion linked to a judgment? Usually when an emotion is linked to a judgment about someone or about a situation, it is revealing an old wound. There is a sense of righteousness about the judgment. You believe in your judgment, and the emotion you are feeling pushes you to react to the outside world. You want to be right. You want to prove your position. You want to project anger and shake up your partner.

This is the case in Situation #1. There are no facts in the situation that can explain the emotion that you are feeling. The source of the emotion lies within you in a wound probably from your childhood. Once you have tagged the emotion to an old wound, you can look inside to discover what the wound is all about. Maybe your father was a strict disciplinarian and you resented that deeply. So when your partner talks about disciplining your children, that brings up the anger you felt with your father when he would discipline you.

In Situation #2, when you consider the facts at hand, your partner's reaction is surprising. There is no apparent cause for your partner's anger. Your partner gets angry and projects his/her anger on you. You feel it in your body. The difference here is in the fact that the emotion, even though you feel it in your body, is not generated from inside of you. Whenever you feel an emotion that seems disconnected from the rest of you, that emotion is probably coming from outside of you. For example, you feel anger in your body yet you have no judgments: your pulse is not rising and you are not projecting it on anyone. Look around. Is there anyone out there that is displaying symptoms of anger? Is anyone screaming or frowning? Is someone addressing you in a curt way or making a disparaging remark? If either one of these exists, the anger you are experiencing in your body may not originate from you.

The intensity of the expression of an emotion is not always in direct proportion to the intensity of feeling that emotion. In other words, someone may be very angry with you and still speak in a low voice and make very subtle negative comments about you. Yet, the intensity of the anger can be tremendous. On the other hand, someone else may scream at you, yet feel a much lesser degree of anger towards you.

In Situation #3, you feel anger as a direct response to an immediate situation, in this case to an aggressive act. You were hit on the arm. Being physically abused is a violation of your personal integrity. The body reacts to defend itself and to do so it generates anger energy. You can use that energy to set up whatever limits are necessary to protect yourself from further violation. This is an example of generating an emotion from a present and immediate situation. As we mentioned earlier, tagging the emotion to its rightful source is key in determining what your response will be to that emotion.

Learning to identify the source of the emotion that you feel in your body is a skill that requires a lot of work. The easier it is for you to identify the source of the emotions that are within you (a wound or a direct response to an immediate reaction), the easier it will be for you to identify sources of emotions that originate outside of yourself.

Dealing with an emotion that is coming from an old wound. As in Situation #1, if the anger you are feeling comes from an old wound, your response should be to go within to uncover and heal that wound. You may choose to share with your partner what you discover. Doing so can increase your emotional intimacy. Even if you share your experience with your partner, the focus for your action remains the source of the emotion itself, in this case, the wound within you. You look within and work on yourself instead of looking without and addressing someone else as the source of what you are feeling.

Dealing with an emotion that comes from someone else. As in Situation #2, if you discover that the anger you are feeling comes from someone else, you may want to ask that person if he or she is feeling the same emotion or you may choose to simply experience the emotion within you. The course of action that you choose depends on your level of acquaintance and intimacy with the person in question. For example, it wouldn't be appropriate to ask a stranger about her feeling even if you are experiencing anger that she is projecting onto you. On the other hand, it could be a synergistic experience to have a similar conversation with a dear friend or with your life partner.

Dealing with an emotion that stems from someone else's action. If the anger you are feeling is a direct and immediate response to the action of someone else as in Situation #3 (you were hit on the arm and you experienced anger), find out the best way to use the energy contained in that emotion. Is it to protect yourself, such as moving away from the person, or is it better to speak with firmness about the fact that you will not tolerate such behaviors?

Use the energy released from you anger and find a creative solution that will work for you and for your relationship.

In all three cases the behavior that you choose will be different, yet the emotion is the same, anger. It's only when you are able to tag the anger to the rightful source that you can find the appropriate solution.

We often use anger as an example to illustrate the importance of tagging an emotion to its rightful source because most people have issues with anger. However, all the situations described above could apply to all the other emotions. For example, you may feel love for someone because of a past experience. You may have loved your father dearly and now you have met a man who has similar physical features. You feel love for that man even though you have no real intimacy with him. This love is coming from within you, from your past and from an association you are making between the appearance of that man and the memory of your father's features and of the love that you had for him. In another example, someone may tell you how much he or she loves you and you feel that love inside of you. Yet, it is not coming from you. Instead, you are receiving his or her love for you and experiencing it in your body. Or someone may give you a hug, and in receiving that hug, you start generating love for that person. The hug has created an immediate response in the present moment. The difference with the preceding example is that the feeling of love that you are experiencing originates within you instead of from the other person.

The more you discover your own emotions and the more you surrender to them and contain them, the easier it will be for you to tag emotions to their rightful source.

Creating emotional intimacy with your partner is about sharing the truth about the emotions you experience. Sharing your emotional experience is not simply naming the emotion; it is also sharing the process of that emotion within you.

What emotion are you feeling? Where does it originate? Does it come from an old wound or from someone else's projection onto you? Or is it the immediate response to a present situation? Are you able to contain it? Are you able to use the energy enclosed in the emotion? What behaviors are you choosing in response to the emotion you are feeling? Are you doing your own inner healing work or are you finding ways to make others responsible for your emotional experience? And if you are doing your own healing work, what work is that?

The more intimate you become with your own emotions and with how you contain and process them, the more you have to share with your partner. Most important, the more you share, the greater the emotional synergy of your relationship. You reveal your heart to each other; its inner workings and its many secrets. As you do this, you increase the level of vulnerability between the two of you. As you become more vulnerable, you learn that it is safe to open your heart and you learn to remove the hidden layers of fear. You discover your partner's gentleness. You learn that you can trust your partner with the hidden wonders of your heart.

Sharing Emotions

Emotions are a beautiful expression of life. Without emotions our life would be bland and without color. Most of us want to feel emotions, but only the "good" ones. We don't want to feel the "bad" ones such as anger, fear, shame and sadness. However, the intensity of your emotions is not something that you can plan or decide. There is no pre-set barometer that you can install in your heart to control the intensity of your emotions. How you use the energy contained in the emotions is the only choice you have.

Emotions are only energy just like thoughts are only energy. You can learn to use that energy to live life fully or you can try to repress it. Unfortunately, if you repress your emotions, it will eventually make you sick literally.

Intimacy in relationships comes from the ability and the willingness to show your heart. We refer to intimacy as INTO-ME-SEE. If you want to enjoy a truly intimate relationship with your partner, you must be willing to feel and to express your emotions along with your emotional process. You can share your thoughts; you can share your daily activities with your partner. But if you want more love in your life, you must share your emotions, your heart.

Some of our clients place a higher value on the mind than on the heart. To them, being rational is more important than being emotional as it puts them in control. Being emotional, on the other hand, makes them vulnerable, and being vulnerable means that they are not in control. Surrendering to your emotions means surrendering to your heart.

The mind does not like to lose control. Whether you like losing control or not has nothing to do with the need to do so. The truth is you need both types of experience to be complete as a human being, and you need both types of experience to be in a genuinely authentic relationship with your partner. That is, you need the experience of the mind, the discernment of the mind; and you need to surrender to emotions, contain emotions and tag them to the right source.

There are many opportunities to create synergy with your partner on the path of the heart. These opportunities reside in the four experiences of emotions or areas of the heart that are listed below. We will discuss how the mastery of each one of those emotional experiences can lead you to greater synergy in your relationship.

Four Experiences of Emotions/Areas of the heart
- Feeling emotions (joy, anger, sadness, fear, excitement, shame and love)
- Expressing emotions (joy, anger, sadness, fear, excitement, shame and love)
- Channeling emotions (joy, anger, sadness, fear, excitement, shame and love)
- Listening to emotions (joy, anger, sadness, fear, excitement, shame and love)

The Canvas of Emotions

In the next section, we will define the specific attributes of the four ways of experiencing emotions: feeling, expressing, channeling and listening to emotions. As we describe these attributes, we won't apply them to all of the emotions available to us as human beings. Instead, we will use a limited number of emotions as examples. When we describe what feeling emotions is about, we may use anger instead of excitement as an example. This is because the process by which we experience emotions is the same for all emotions.

Since we will not be reviewing all of the emotions for all the different ways of experiencing emotions, we will use a simple canvas of emotions. As mentioned earlier, this canvas includes anger, joy, sadness, shame, love, fear and excitement. These emotions are the basic ones from which spring all other forms of emotion. For example, feeling ecstatic is a stronger form of joy, and feeling enraged is a stronger form of anger. All other emotions are a variation or a degree of a basic emotion. It's a little bit like acknowledging the existence of the primary colors and then creating different ones by increasing or decreasing the concentration of pigmentation or by combining different colors.

We have found that reducing the number of emotions down to the primary ones helps our clients identify them. Because of the difficulty that most people have in naming emotions, by simplifying the emotional nomenclature, our clients can focus more easily on what they are feeling in their hearts.

Emotional Default Position

Before we venture into each emotion, let's look at your emotional default position.

What is an emotional default position? Each of us has an emotional default position. An emotional default position is the emotion that you go back to when no other emotion is being generated either from within or from outside of yourself. Have you noticed how some people always seem to be happy whereas others always seem to be depressed? Have you ever wondered why that is? It is because they have different emotional default positions. Emotional default positions are learned. We develop them as children by identifying with our main source of emotional support.

Let's look at an example. If you identified your mother as the emotional support system in your family, you started identifying with her emotional default position. Was your mother a joyous person or someone who was constantly depressed? If your mother was in a constant state of depression, you were fed that depression. You took into your body the feelings of sadness and of hopelessness that constitute depression. Gradually you started generating for yourself feelings that were originally generated from your mother. That is, you generated the same emotion that you were fed by your mother. You learned from your mother that your "natural" state of emotional being would be depression. Her emotional default position became your emotional default position.

Move forward 20 years. When you are not consciously creating another emotion in your life or when someone else or something else is not sourcing that for you, you notice that you easily become depressed. You wonder why. You are depressed because your emotional default position is depression.

We believe that because so many of us have negative emotional default positions such as anger, fear, depression or shame, many of us look for outside stimulants to cover up those unpleasant emotions or to find other sources of positive emotions. Not having learned to generate joy, excitement and love from within, we look for outside sources. We now "need" to buy the latest fashions or to follow the newest trends. We "need" to fall in love or to seek sexual escapades. We "need" to buy the most recent car or the gadget of the week. All of this involves looking outside of ourselves for a new emotional default position.

The good news is that since your emotional default position is learned behavior, you can change it. However, it requires a lot of patience and a great deal of work. An emotional default position is not developed around one traumatic event. It is slowly built around years of living in a certain emotional environment. After being fed a specific emotion every day for a great number of years eventually, it became your modus operandi. To transform your learned position, you have to do extensive healing work. That work combines the discovery of the beliefs you hold about your life and about yourself as well as re-experiencing the emotional programming that you took on from your main emotional support person.

The first step is to ask, who were your emotional models, what beliefs did you take on from them about emotions? What did that feel as a child? Re-experiencing the daily occurrence of being fed a specific emotion and acknowledging that as the source of your current default position goes a long way towards enabling you to make a different choice.

One of our clients' emotional default position was numbness. He learned as a child that he shouldn't feel any emotions. The expression of all emotions was banned from his life. He watched his parents submit to strict religious dogmas that enforced a strict work ethic and prohibited all manifestations of excitement, joy and love. Needless to say, his was not an affectionate and nurturing environment. In order to transform his life and reset his emotional default position, he had to re-experience the numbness that he was fed every day as a child. He had to question the beliefs that he had taken on such as, What I feel doesn't count! What I want is not important! The only thing that is important is to do the task at hand! He had to relive the incredible sadness that he felt at being constantly shut down. Only when he had allowed enough of that pain to resurface, when he had questioned and denounced the beliefs that shut him down, was he able to choose a different emotional default position.

What is your emotional default position? Where did you learn it? What emotional default position do you want for yourself? Do you want to create joy or love as your emotional default position? Choosing to do so is the first step in transforming your position.

The second step consists of healing the beliefs and the emotional habits that you took on. If you are easily depressed or seem to live in constant fear, you don't need to live that way. All it takes is the willingness to do your own inner healing work and to maintain the vision of what you want to create. Visualize your new emotional default position. Imagine what life would be like if you lived it from a perspective of joy and of love. Believe in your ability to create the emotional experience that you want for yourself.

The Basic Human Emotions

Let's look at the basic emotions in our human experience: anger, joy, sadness, shame, love, fear and excitement.

Anger. Anger is the emotion and the expression of the creation process. It is the emotion that holds aggressive energy. Remember back to your childhood when your anger showed up. You usually felt and expressed anger when you wanted to affirm an opinion or when you wanted to have your way. You were trying to "create" what you wanted for yourself. You were affirming your will. You confronted the obstacles to getting what you wanted with words or physical deeds. In brief, you used your anger/energy to break down the obstacles to having what you wanted.

Your ability to feel and express anger is intimately linked to the ability to be creative. Anger energy enables us to change the course of a situation. It can do so in the outside world when you confront someone and can do so in your internal world when you confront your own limitations with vigor or break through an inner resistance to creativity.

Anger can be a healthy expression of your creative energy. However, it must be expressed in a responsible way. Sharing your anger without projecting its energy is the key to expressing it responsibly. You own the energy contained in the anger, yet you share the reality of it. In doing so, you increase the level of synergy with your partner. This is the difference between screaming at someone and sharing calmly that you are feeling anger.

Repressed anger can make you sick; literally. Because anger is creative in nature, it needs to be tackled and directed towards positive outlets. If it is repressed, it becomes destructive, it literally turns on the person that is repressing it. The symptoms of repressed anger can range from chronic resentment and a pessimistic attitude towards life to low physical stamina and depleted energy including different forms of physical ailments and disease.

Almost everyone has issues with anger. People either have trouble feeling it, expressing it or listening to it. They most certainly have trouble channeling it. Why is that? Since anger represents the ability to create and the will to choose and to decide, it often manifests as a confrontation with someone else's will. Unless your parents had achieved a high level of creativity in their life, reached their goals and tackled their level of anger, seeing their child display anger was often viewed as a personal confrontation.

Your parents probably learned to repress their own anger. Seeing you express your own freely confronted them with their own personal limitations so you had to be shut down. While not consciously able to nurture their own creative process, they stifled their children's creative process.

Joy. Joy is the emotion and the expression of the life force within. It is one of those "preferred" emotions. Everyone wants to experience joy. If we had a choice, joy along with love and excitement would probably be the only emotions that we would choose. The experience of joy is usually tied to an experience of well-being in the present moment. When you experience joy, your energy level is high, you have an open attitude towards others and your vision of life is positive. You feel "good."

You can also experience joy in the present moment because of success or good fortune in certain areas of your life. This is joy that comes from outside. Because joy in this case is sourced from outside of yourself, it can also be destroyed by what is outside of yourself. As a result, this type of joy is illusive and transitory. It comes and goes with the fluctuations of your life. When you are successful, when people are nice to you, when the stock exchange is doing well, you experience joy.

But joy does not have to be a transitory emotion; it can be experienced on a more permanent basis. In fact, it can be your emotional default position. Joy can be linked to your state of being. That type of joy is not tied to the events of your life. You are joyous simply because you are. This type of joy is accessible when most of your healing work is done.

Sadness. Sadness is the emotion and the expression of separation and of grief. You feel sadness when you lose someone you love or when you leave the friends you made at your old job to take on a new position in another city. In both these instances, you are letting go of people you love or are close to, of an environment that you have come to cherish and appreciate. Experiencing separation is a natural phenomenon. We all go through some form of separation. Separation can be brought on by life's natural cycles such as the death of a loved one or the move to a new home or a new job. You can also create separation through your own free choice such as in the case of a divorce or of parting ways with a friend. In all of those situations separation occurs whether or not they are occurrences outside of your control or of your own volition.

With separation comes grief. When you grieve, your heart acknowledges the emotional attachment you had with the person or situation you are leaving. Your heart is acknowledging the love you feel. Once it has acknowledged the love you feel, your heart can let go. Your sadness expresses that letting go. The tears that you cry and the pain that you feel are the expression of your heart surrendering that attachment. When you allow yourself to fully experience sadness, you create space in your heart for a new form of attachment.

Sadness is a transitory emotion. It shouldn't be chosen as an emotional default position. People who are constantly sad learned that behavior as children. If their sadness is not based on some form of separation that is occurring in their life at the time, it is an automatic response to life, an emotional default position. Healing work such as prescribed earlier should be pursued.

Shame. Shame is an exception in this list of basic emotion. Shame is not only an emotion, it is a syndrome: a combination of fear with a series of negative beliefs about one's self. For example, you may hold the belief that you are bad, flawed or unlovable and you fear being found out. The fear is crystallized with the belief that there is something intrinsically wrong with you.

Shame is pervasive. It seems that everyone has one form of shame or another.

Shame usually lies hidden under other emotions. It may be hidden under sadness or anger, or it may be hidden under a deflective sense of humor. That is, you laugh at yourself because you cannot bear to feel the shame that is hidden behind it. One of our clients easily talked about her childhood wounds using the phrase "Isn't this ridiculous." She would then proceed to describe with a great deal of humor a horrific childhood experience. She had learned to protect herself from her shame by making fun of it.

Shame can manifests itself through the following beliefs:
- I'm flawed
- I'm inferior
- I fall short as a human being
- I'm basically unlovable
- I'm inadequate
- I'm a failure
- I'm bad
- I have contempt for myself
- I'm worthless

I'm Right...You Need to Change

Those beliefs are so deeply ingrained in our minds that we are convinced they are true. When you have such beliefs about yourself, the behaviors you exhibit will probably be one of the following:
- Extreme embarrassment
- Extreme shyness
- Extreme humility
- Trying to protect yourself from others
- Trying to hide yourself from others
- Fear of being vulnerable
- Fear of someone finding out who you really are
- Shutting down so as to avoid feelings of hopelessness
- Sense of emptiness
- Scrutinizing every behavior, resulting in paralysis causing passivity and inaction
- Numbed with food, drugs, alcohol or sex to avoid feelings
- Confusion between what you did and who you are
- Blaming others so as not to feel your own pain
- Perceiving that you are being controlled
- Fear of being out of control (avoiding new situation)
- Apologizing constantly
- Negative self-talk
- Constantly questioning past choices (actions and behaviors)
- Self-sabotage
- Reluctant to change
- Perfectionist and workaholic to prove that you are capable and adequate
- Underachiever from fear of failure

Shame results from different causes. It can occur as early as in the preverbal stage of life. In fact, shame is energy and can be absorbed without ever knowing it. For example, your parents may have looked at you with contempt when you were a baby, and somehow you registered that to mean you were bad. Constant criticism, constant hostility may have been a major part of your childhood. Or you may have been rejected by your parents and have experienced them withdrawing their love for you. Your parents may have held high standards of behavior and may have reacted with anger when you did not live up to those standards. You may have been punished for crying, for being in pain or for being in distress. Your peers may have ridiculed or teased you cruelly. Your parents may have been harsh disciplinarians. You may have endured physical or sexual abuse. You may have also taken on your parent's shame. Your parents may have been co-dependent emotionally (putting you in the role of the wife or of the husband). These are some of the countless causes of shame.

Do any of them seem familiar? When you review the list, is it any wonder that almost everyone experiences one form of shame or another? As you were subjected to such behaviors from your parents, you took on beliefs about yourself and you started acting out with shame. In the process you lost your real sense of self. Shame is not about what you do; it is about who you are. That is much more devastating because it is much easier to change a behavior (what you do) than it is to heal negative beliefs about yourself (who you are).

In order to heal shame, you must accept that it exists and that you have it within you. You must also be willing to re-experience the childhood events that created the experience of shame within you. We believe that shame is a great teacher for compassion. That is, people who have successfully healed their own shame are much more careful about the images, beliefs and emotions they carry about others. They are much more gentle with others' shortcomings and shameful behaviors. Because most people experience some form of shame and because it is often hidden under other emotions, we have included it into our basic emotional canvas.

Love. Love is the emotion and expression of synergy. Love is the emotion that links us to other people, to things and experiences in life. You love your children. You have a bond to them. You are connected to them. You hold them in your heart. You can also love your home. You cherish the time you spend there, and in that way you hold it in your heart.

With love comes understanding of the heart. When you are in a state of love for someone, you understand who they really are, and you are sensitive to their emotions and their dreams. Being in a state of love is very different from falling in love or from being in love. When you fall in love, you are attracted by the qualities that you believe are in the other person. Although there is no real emotional intimacy yet, the attraction is strong and irresistible. You believe the person can do no wrong. You are mesmerized by who she or he is. You have idealized the person. You love the idea of the other person.

To love someone, you need to know him or her deeply. You not only accept who the person is, you also honor his or her positive and negative attributes. You embrace in your heart the person's light side and shadow parts. Loving someone results from greater emotional intimacy. To love is both an emotion and a choice. You choose to keep your heart open and to hold the other person in your love consciousness.

Love heals, forgives and nurtures all who come in contact with it. Love makes a wonderful emotional default position. In fact, we believe that love and joy are the natural emotional default positions that we are all born with. However, as a child you may have learned differently by what you observed and by what you absorbed in your body. You may have learned to live in fear or in shame. Or you were fortunate to have parents who did their own healing work. As a result, love and joy may be your emotional default positions.

Fear. Fear is the emotion and the expression of change and discovery. We experience fear when we are uncertain about an outcome or when we project a specific outcome. Fear always precedes a discovery. We fear that we have cancer. We don't know yet if we do, but we are afraid that we might. Or we fear death. We are not experiencing death but we are afraid of the experience of death. Or we are afraid of financial hardship. We may not be experiencing hardship at the present time but our fear is tied to the future.

Fear is rarely linked to a present situation. It is usually projected on something that will happen, not on something that is happening in the present moment. Nevertheless, fear can be a real emotion tied to a real threat. For example, you may walk home at night and glance down a dark street; you may experience fear and choose a different route. In this case, your fear may have saved your life. Your fear may have been warranted, there may have been a real danger down that dark street.

Fear is a useful emotion in that it can help you know instinctively where real danger lurks as in the above example. So you must listen to your fear and determine if it is based on facts or if it is an expression of your uncertainty about a change in your life and about discovering something new and different.

Most of us function from our Ego. As we discussed earlier, the Ego is a survival structure that we set in place unconsciously as children in order to understand and to survive. The Ego dislikes change and automatically generates fear when it perceives the possibility of change. Sometimes we experience this as being afraid to try out for a new job or being afraid to meet new people. You may experience fear when someone tries to point out something that you do that doesn't work. Every situation that brings about a new discovery of Self, every person who unveils a new part of yourself that your Ego is not comfortable with will bring about fear.

Fear is normal. Welcome it. Then look at the facts. Is there a real situation that warrants the fear? Are you in real danger? Or is the fear a product of your thoughts, of your judgments and beliefs about an upcoming event? In the latter case, know in your heart that your fear is Ego based. Simply feel it through your body and let it go. The fear that you are experiencing is a signal that you are moving on to the discovery of more of yourself. Celebrate it!!!

Excitement. Excitement is the emotion and the expression of motivation. You experience excitement when you are venturing on an unknown path for your life. You may have experienced excitement when you started reading this book, hoping that it will help you transform your relationship. Let's hope that excitement has grown as you move from chapter to chapter.

You may experience excitement when you start a new project, especially if it is related to your dream, your vision. Excitement energy is released when you are motivated to pursue a dream. No matter what the dream is, your motivation can be high and so will your excitement level. But holding a dream in your mind is not sufficient to bring it about. The thought of the dream must be infused

I'm Right...You Need to Change

with your excitement, the reason that motivates you into action; the benefits that you strive to reach.

We all carry excitement differently. Some people are powerful carriers of excitement, apparently excited about everything. For others, it takes a lot to bring about any feeling of excitement. Are you a good carrier of excitement or is this an emotion that you don't often experience?

To help answer these questions, once again look to the models in your life and notice if excitement was part of your daily emotional regime. If not, chances are that your natural expression of excitement was stifled. Based on this insight, revisit your beliefs about excitement. You may have a belief that excitement is not okay. Maybe you believe that adults should never get excited, that excitement is a sign of immaturity. You may discover that one of the messages you heard as a child was: "Don't get so excited!" or "Will you please calm down!"

Re-experience what those messages felt like in your body. Remember the specific events in your childhood that led you to shut down your excitement. Re-experience the pain of those experiences. Excitement can be a healthy emotional default position. You may want to experience life that way. Can you imagine being excited about life every day? Can you imagine being excited about the small things in life? Being excited about going to the coffee shop with a friend? Being excited about going to the movies? Being excited about going grocery shopping? Can you imagine the impact on your physical level of energy and on your health? Can you imagine the impact on your relationship? Suddenly you become a willing participant in life. Your excitement is infectious, and your partner will be more than willing to share it with you.

The Areas of Synergy in Your Relationship/ The Four Experiences of Emotions

As mentioned earlier, each of the emotions described above can be experienced in four different ways: feeling, expressing, channeling and listening

Feeling Emotions

We can experience our emotions by feeling them. As mentioned earlier, we are not referring to the simple fact of naming an emotion. We are referring to the actual feeling of the emotion as in "surrendering to the emotion." When you feel your emotion, you are in your emotion. You become your emotion. You feel it in your body.

When you feel your emotion, you don't know where the beginning or the end of it is. You release your resistance to feeling it and allow the energy to run through your body. When you truly feel your emotion, you lose track of time and space and simply allow it to take over.

Feeling your emotions is an individual experience. All of us have "favorite" or "preferred" emotions. These are the emotions that we like feeling. Generally, you like feeling love, joy and excitement. It may even be easy for you to feel sadness, whereas anger may be difficult for you to access. No matter what emotion you have trouble feeling, your inability to do so will affect the level of synergy of your relationship.

Let's take an example. You have trouble feeling your anger. As a child you learned that good girls never get angry. Years later, when your partner does something that irritates you, you dismiss your anger. After a while, you start noticing that you have less joy in your life, that you feel less love for your partner. You may even experience a loss of sexual attraction to your partner. What happened?

Your inability to feel your anger has paralyzed your ability to feel "any" emotion. In order for you to experience a different emotion, you must release the emotion that you are having in the present by allowing yourself to experience it. In the path of the heart, no judgment is made on emotions. Each emotion is energy that must be felt. When you refuse to feel one emotion, it stifles your ability to feel the others. To create greater intimacy with your partner, therefore, you have to learn to feel all of your emotions.

We get our first lessons in feeling as children. As such, we learn in many different ways, as discussed below.

We learn to feel through observation. As small children, we have no problem feeling our emotions, but as we begin to develop in consciousness, we learn to restrict our feeling abilities. We learn that joy can be felt but not excitement, or that anger should not be felt.

What were the models in your life when you learned about feeling emotions? Did your parents share their emotions with you? Did they encourage you to feel your own emotions? Did they validate the emotions that you were feeling or did they tell you that certain emotions were wrong, as in "It's wrong to feel anger." What did your parents do with the emotions that they felt? Were they honest about their emotions or did they try to hide them? Bring back your childhood memories. What messages did you receive about feeling emotions? If you don't have easy access to your childhood memories, notice if your parents are able in the present to share their experience of feeling emotions.

We learn to feel through experience. How did you experience the anger of your parents? Did they throw their anger at you? Did they act out their anger at you or did you watch others being hurt by their anger? What was your experience of anger as a child? How did you experience sadness as a child? Did you watch your parents express their sadness and making it okay to do so, or did you experience their sadness as heart wrenching? Was sadness experienced as a normal expression of being human or was it repressed and held back? How did you experience the sadness around you as a child?

Your ability to feel your emotions as an adult is a direct result of what you observed and experienced as a child. If feeling joy was okay but feeling fear was not, you probably believe that joy is a "good" emotion and you most certainly consider fear a "bad" emotion.

We all feel emotions; we have no choice. We feel emotions; our choice is about consciousness. Do you choose to be conscious of what you are feeling or do you choose to be unconscious of your emotions?

If you want to create intimacy with your partner, you must be able to open your heart to him or her. Opening your heart is not only about opening to love. The heart expresses all the other emotions as well. Opening your heart to your partner is about revealing all of your emotions.

Emotional intimacy with another starts with emotional intimacy with one's Self. If you have trouble sharing your emotions with your partner, look within. Scrutinize your beliefs about your emotions. Which are the "good" and the "bad" emotions? Where did you learn to feel the way you do? Who were your models? What emotions are you good at feeling? Which ones do you shy away from?

You won't be able to open your heart to your partner if you cannot open your heart to yourself. How can you share your sadness with your partner if you don't allow yourself to feel it within yourself? How can you share your excitement around a project or a vision if you can't even feel the excitement within you?

Choosing to experience emotional intimacy with your partner implies that you are willing to re-educate yourself. The beliefs that you took on such as "anger is bad" must be denounced for what they are as they hinder your experience of your Self. They cut you off from a part of yourself and in doing so, they cut you off from enjoying a deep connection with your partner. Reinforce the beliefs that increase your experience of your Self, such as "It's okay to feel all of my emotions," and denounce those that limit that experience, such as "Anger is a bad emotion and shouldn't be felt." If I feel it, there must be something wrong with me."

Make a declaration that you are willing to feel all of your emotions. The power of our intentions never ceases to amaze us. What you intend in your mind and in your heart always happens. When you declare your intention to the world, when you declare that you are willing to feel all of your emotions, suddenly, events and people start showing up in your life that enable you to actualize your intention. You will start noticing your emotions more and more. You may even attract people in your life that trigger strong emotions

I'm Right...You Need to Change

in you. These emotions are yours. These people are not responsible for your experience.

Emotions stem from within. Others serve as triggers to bring them out. Notice how different people react differently to similar events or the same individual. Where do those differences come from? They come from the fact that our emotions are our own. They come from the fact that through the course of our life, we have connected different emotions to similar events. People are simply there to remind us of the beliefs we have about life and to help us resurface the emotions we have attached around those beliefs.

Let's take an example. You learned early on that expressing sadness was a sign of weakness. For example, you watched your father hold in his sadness when his mother died, and you watched him repress his pain when he lost his best friend to cancer. You loved your father dearly; he was your hero, so you modeled your behavior after his, deciding that sadness should never be felt. Now move to the present. Your partner expresses his or her sadness easily. As a child, he or she learned that it was okay to feel sadness. Every time that happens you have a judgment that your partner is weak. Somewhere in your subconscious you made a decision about feeling sadness, and you are now projecting that decision on to your partner.

Notice what your reaction is when people express their emotions. What emotion do you react to? What decision did you make about feeling that emotion? Own that reaction. Your reaction to the person expressing a particular emotion says a lot more about you than it says about the person. Use your reaction to discover your beliefs about feeling emotions. Commit to re-educating yourself.

As you do so, reinforce the belief that feeling emotions is a positive skill, encourage it, and practice. The more you develop your ability to feel, the easier it will be for you to decide to move on to the next experience of emotions expressing your emotions. You cannot express an emotion that you do not feel. The more you develop the ability to feel your emotions, the easier it will be for you to share them with your partner. Remember intimacy is about letting the other INTO-ME-SEE.

Expressing Emotions

Emotions don't always have to be expressed. Learning to discern when it is appropriate to express an emotion and when it is not is critical if your goal is to create synergy with your partner. When you feel an emotion and you want to express it, check to be sure that doing so creates positive synergy with your partner. If the answer is yes, then share it. Sharing loving feelings joy or excitement usually increases the synergy with one's partner. Remember, emotions are contagious. You want to infect your partner with your positive emotions just as you want to be infected.

On the other hand, if sharing the emotion that you are feeling does not in and of itself create positive synergy as in the case of anger, look at your intention. Why do you want to share that emotion? Is it because it is lingering and you need to reveal it to let it go?

If that's the case, state that as your intention to your partner and share your emotion. However, if your intention in sharing the emotion is to make your partner wrong, if your intention is "to give it back to her or him," hold on to your emotion, look within, do your own inner healing work. Look at what wound is driving you to such an intention. Only when your intention is to increase synergy with your partner should you share your emotion.

You may also be able to let go of an emotion that doesn't create synergy such as anger and fear by simply letting it go. If you believe that you can let go of such an emotion without sharing it, do so; however, make sure that you are not repressing your emotion. For example, you experience anger at what your partner said. It is no big thing, so you decide to let it go. You know that you often react that way. You understand the wound behind it. Later on during the day, you become snappy with your partner for no apparent reason. You criticize your partner's choice of restaurant and you feel edgy. When you start looking within, you come to the realization you are still holding on to the anger that you experienced earlier in the day. In this situation, you thought you could let go of the anger but you didn't. You repressed it instead. So if you decide to let go of an emotion such as fear or anger, make sure that you are truly letting it go.

I'm Right...You Need to Change

Repression vs, projection. Most people either repress their emotions or project them on to others. When you repress your emotion, you push it down; you hide it in your body. Repressing is a refusal to be conscious. It's pretending that something is not there and refusing to experience it. However, when you refuse to experience the emotion, your body carries it. For example, you start feeling fear; you instantly start thinking of reasons for not feeling fear and you move your emotion aside. Yet, the fear is still there. You have buried it in your body.

It is easy to read the body of those who repress their emotions. People with repressed anger often have a body that is shut down, manifesting a rigid gait, and experiencing tightness or pain in specific parts of their body. Some of them wear a perpetual frown. People with repressed fear often look askance. Their eyes reflect the fear that they are holding in their bodies.

If an emotion is repressed, it does not disappear. It remains in the body waiting for an opportunity to show up. And it usually shows up in inappropriate ways. We call this expressing emotions "sideways."

Let's use an example to illustrate. Your partner is late, and because of his late arrival, the dinner is overcooked. You are angry. Instead of expressing your anger in a responsible way when he comes home, you decide to repress it. You decide that your partner has had a rough day and you don't want to burden him or her further.

Later on in the evening, you start talking about the children. You don't agree about how they should be disciplined. Instead of looking at the facts of the situation and evaluating the real needs of the children, you start attacking your partner by pointing out his (your perceived) failures as a parent. You may say, "Don't you talk to me about discipline, you are never there to enforce it, you are always late for supper," "Where's your own discipline?" "I'm the one who is always there to take care of them, I'll decide what they need." Suddenly, the discussion about discipline has become a discussion about your partner's shortcomings. Why and how did this happen?

It happened because you did not honor your anger when it originally showed up. Remember when your partner came home and you decided not to tell him how you felt? You did not express your anger when it showed up and you didn't let it go either. You bottled it up in your body and later it came out sideways.

"Sideways" is an expression that we use to mean that the emotion felt and repressed in the past is showing up in situations where it has no relevance. For example, the anger you felt when your partner was late is not related to your discussion about discipline. Yet, that's where it showed up. Repressed emotions reinforce judgments that you are holding in your mind about a situation. In brief, emotions do not disappear when you repress them. They only disappear when you accept/honor that you have them, when you feel them and when you express them in a responsible way.

If you want to create intimacy with your partner, you must consciously choose to express emotions. Remember, there are two types of emotions that you want to express. You want to express all of your positive emotions. You want to infect your partner with your love, joy and excitement and you want the same for yourself. You also want to express the negative emotions (anger, fear, shame and sadness) that you cannot let go and that you want to share with the purpose of healing and creating greater synergy.

Ways of expressing emotions. Now that we know what emotions to express, let's talk about how to express them. There are two ways to express emotions.

1. Projecting your emotion on to the other. For example, you feel anger at your partner and start screaming. When you do this, you are giving away the energy that is contained in your emotion. Usually your partner will respond in kind. When we project our anger, we are oftentimes trying to be right. We see the other as the cause of our anger and we come up with all kinds of judgments. Our emotion becomes the fuel with which we try to prove our point. This creates separation and is totally useless in coming up with an appropriate solution. In short, projecting your negative emotions on your partner does not work. It creates separation.

Positive emotions are a different story altogether. You want to project your positive emotions on your partner. You want to share the love you feel for your partner along with the joy and

I'm Right...You Need to Change

the excitement that you experience in life. Remember the positive emotional infection!!!

2. Expressing emotions in a responsible way. This is the best way to communicate negative emotions. Instead of projecting the energy contained in your emotion, you contain it within yourself and simply name it. In your mind, you do not hold your partner responsible for your emotion. You are simply sharing your emotion. For example, you are feeling anger about something your partner did. You feel the anger, you contain it within yourself, you allow it to move through your body and you inform your partner that you are feeling anger. You do not blame your partner for your emotion. You simply share the fact of your emotion. By acting this way, you become responsible in your behavior for the emotion you are experiencing.

All of our emotions emanate from our being. Other people act as triggers that enable us to feel specific emotions. They are not responsible for what we feel. We are responsible. Even when others project negative emotions on us and become the originators of the emotion we are feeling, our experience of the emotion is our own and varies from one person to the next.

Once again, remember how different individuals react differently to the same person or situation. This is because we hold within ourselves the key to how we experience emotions. We call this the button-pushing theory. Imagine that all your emotions can be called forth by pressing an individualized set of buttons. You are the only one with this set of buttons. When someone speaks or acts, what they do or say pushes specific buttons. Since you are the only one with those particular buttons, you may be the only one who reacts. How you experience emotions is your own individual reality. No one has the same identical emotional experience.

When you have learned to express your emotions in a responsible way, you can start using the energy released by the emotion and direct it to a creative end. This is what we call channeling emotions.

In order to create greater intimacy with your partner you need to:
- discern between the emotions that create synergy in and of themselves

- learn to express your emotions such as anger and fear in a responsible way
- learn to project the charge of emotions such as love, joy and excitement to your partner

Emotional synergy with your partner increases when both of you learn to infect each other with positive emotions such as love, joy and excitement. It also increases when you share your anger, sadness and fear in a responsible way.

Channeling Emotions

Few people know how to channel emotions in a conscious way. Why is that? Before we can channel the energy contained in our emotions, we must have mastered the ability to feel them and to express them responsibly. That is, the energy will not be unleashed from the emotion until you honor it by acknowledging its existence, until you surrender to feeling it through your body and choose to express it in a responsible way.

Let's look at an example. You are angry at your partner for not picking up the kids at school. You acknowledge the emotion in your body and decide to share it with your partner. You contain it and do not project it onto your partner. Instead, you make a conscious choice to hold your emotional energy and to feel it inside your body. You let go of wanting to be right. If your emotion is contained, you use the energy to look at the facts with your partner. Is this a recurring problem or an isolated occurrence? Do you need to come up with a solution? If that's the case, you and your partner can identify a solution that serves both your needs and those of your children, in this case. A contained emotion releases energy that you can use to find a solution.

Let's revisit this example. Same situation, however, this time, you blame your partner and start projecting your anger. You end up blaming each other. There is no solution. Both partners to prove the righteousness of their position have used the anger/energy. The energy has not been channeled in a constructive and conscious way. The anger linked up with a judgment and was projected on to the other.

Channeling emotions is a powerful way to create synergy between partners. If both partners are able to consciously channel the energy contained in their emotions, they can focus on their vision and their goals and use the energy to create what they want in their life.

Let's look at another example. You and your partner are frustrated about your financial situation. You are barely making ends meet. You decide to use the anger and frustration that you are feeling to find a solution. You express the emotions that you are feeling and use that energy to find creative ways to generate more money. That is, instead of focusing your emotional energy on blaming each other or blaming the stock market or the economy, you focus the energy on what you can do. You are consciously channeling the energy contained in your emotions together.

This is the creative process at work. An idea gives you an image of what you want to create. The energy contained in an emotion acts as a fuel to enable you to actualize it.

To create greater intimacy with your partner, you have to learn for yourself how to channel the energy released by your emotions. Once you have developed that skill, you can practice it with your partner. Channeling emotional energy with your partner brings about numerous rewards, you are more creative, you reach your goals more easily, you experience being empowered both individually and as a couple and you learn to turn adversity into incredible opportunities for success. What a wonderful way to strengthen the ties that bind you and to increase the synergy in your relationship!!!

Listening to Emotions

Your ability to listen to others express their emotions is a direct reflection of your ability to feel and to express your own. Individuals who have trouble listening to certain emotions usually have trouble feeling and expressing those same emotions.

For example, if you have difficulty feeling excitement about life, you will have trouble listening to your partner's excitement. What usually happens in a situation such as this is that the partner who has difficulty feeling and expressing excitement will attempt to dampen the excitement of the other partner. He or she will come up with reasons why an idea or project won't work. Fear will slowly replace the initial excitement. As a result, one partner's inadequacy at feeling an emotion sabotages the expression of the other partner's emotion.

Which of the emotions do you have trouble listening to? Is it anger? Do you cringe when your partner shares anger? Is it fear? Do you try to comfort your partner when fear is expressed? Learn to simply listen to the expression of emotions. Observe what is happening inside of you. Does the expression of a particular emotion create a reaction? If so, what is that reaction?

The reaction you experience when listening to your partner's emotion is yours. It has nothing to do with your partner's emotion. Learn to control your mind, especially the "fixer" mind. When your partner is sad, do you try to console? Do you offer solution to take the sadness away? Do you say comments such as "It's not so bad, you'll feel better later" or "Don't worry, you'll find another job."

We notice during our coaching sessions that one partner often tries to "fix" the other. They are uncomfortable with the "painful" emotion that their partner is experiencing. When that happens, we support them in looking at what is going on inside themselves. What button is being pushed? In most cases, if you have trouble listening to an emotion, it is a sign of an unhealed emotion inside of you.

Learn to listen with your mind. Validate the fact of the emotion. Accept and honor that your partner is feeling the way that he/she is. Also learn to feel the emotional charge in your body. How does it feel when your partner is expressing an emotion? What does joy feel like in your body when your partner expresses it? What does anger feel like in your body?

And finally, learn to receive the emotion in your heart. Open up to empathy. Learn to vibrate to the same emotional frequency as your partner. Open up to feeling what your partner is feeling. Be totally open, let go of your own emotions and focus on getting your partner's emotions. Choose to be present by separating yourself from your experience and being attentive to your partner's emotional expression.

Listening is not about repressing what you feel. It is about holding in check what you feel and think. It is a little like containing your experience in a separate room while maintaining an awareness of what is going on. The more you learn to be totally present for your partner as you maintain an awareness of your own, the greater your ability to be intimate with your partner. You learn to be there emotionally for your partner.

The ability to listen to your partner's emotions will greatly increase the synergy of your relationship. The simple act of listening does wonders for validating the other's experience. We all need to be validated, to experience that our partner really "gets" our experience without judgment or interpretation. In so doing, we create a safe space for both partners to be authentic, and we increase the intimacy of our hearts.

YOUR SYNERGY CHECKLIST

REMEMBER:
You can increase your synergy on the path of the heart if you:
- Feel and express your anger together in a responsible way
- Feel and express your joy together in a responsible way
- Feel and express your sadness together in a responsible way
- Feel and express your shame together in a responsible way
- Feel and express your love together in a responsible way
- Feel and express your fear together in a responsible way
- Feel and express your excitement together in a responsible way
- Channel your anger together in a constructive way
- Channel your joy together in a constructive way
- Channel your sadness together in a constructive way
- Channel your shame together in a constructive way
- Channel your love together in a constructive way
- Channel your fear together in a constructive way
- Channel your excitement together in a constructive way
- Listen to each other's anger without taking it personally
- Listen to each other's joy
- Listen to each other's sadness without taking it personally
- Listen to each other's shame without taking it personally
- Listen to each other's love
- Listen to each other's fear without taking it personally
- Listen to each other's excitement

How's your synergy doing?
Now, let's take a look at how Ron and I handled our journey on the path of the heart.

Our Journey on the Path of the Heart

When Ron and I first got together, we had done a lot of work in the dimension of the heart. We were both able to feel and to express our emotions to others. However, expressing your emotions to friends and to acquaintances is very different from expressing them in an intimate relationship, especially when part of you thinks that the other is the source of a given emotion. Even with the extensive training that we had, we encountered our share of challenges as we endeavored to open our hearts more and more to each other. Surrendering to our emotions and containing our emotions was relatively easy for both of us, but expressing emotions such as anger and sadness presented more of a challenge. In our practice as transformational coaches we have observed that anger along with shame and fear are often the most difficult emotions for couples to express. And so it was for us.

To illustrate our journey we have used two tables. The first illustrates how we fare in terms of feeling our emotions. Feeling emotions is an individual experience and therefore cannot easily be observed by the other partner. For this reason, it is difficult to evaluate the level of synergy between partners in this area. The terms used to assess the ability to feel are different from those we used on the Synergy Continuum. To assess our ability to feel emotions, we use the words "able" to indicate an ease at feeling emotions and "unable" to indicate difficulty at feeling emotions. The second column indicates our level of ability at the beginning of our relationship and the third column shows our level of ability after we did our individual work and our couple's work. We will now go through each one of these areas.

Feeling Our Emotions

Areas of the Heart/Emotions	Synergy Level at the Beginning of Our Relationship	Synergy Level After We Did Our Healing Work
Feeling our anger	Ron – unable Danyelle – able	Ron – able Danyelle - able.
Feeling our joy	Ron – unable Danyelle – able	Ron – unable Danyelle – able
Feeling our sadness	Ron – able Danyelle – able	Ron – able Danyelle – able
Feeling our shame	Ron – able Danyelle – able	Ron – able Danyelle – able
Feeling our love	Ron – able Danyelle – able	Ron – able Danyelle – able
Feeling our fear	Ron – able Danyelle – able	Ron – able Danyelle – able
Feeling our excitement	Ron – unable Danyelle – able	Ron – able Danyelle – able

The second table illustrates our synergy levels of expressing, channeling and listening to emotions. The second column indicates our initial level of synergy the level of synergy we experienced when we first got together. The third column shows how that level evolved after we did our individual and our couple's work.

We use the model presented in Chapter 2 to assess our synergy levels. As you will recall, there are four levels to choose from: contempt, disagreement, accept/honor and agree. When we either "accept/honor" or "agree with" our partner's position, we create synergy. Of these two, agreement creates the greater synergy. When we "disagree with" or are "in contempt for" each other's position, on the other hand, we create separation in the relationship. Of those two, being in contempt creates the greater separation.

You will notice that we did not experience contempt for any of the areas on the path of the heart. This is a result of the work that we had done prior to getting together as a couple. Moving from separation to synergy was a challenge for us in some of the areas, however, but it also became a wonderful experience in self-healing. We will be discussing each one of those areas in the following pages.

Expressing, Channeling and Listening to Our Emotions

Areas of the Heart/Emotions	Synergy Level at the Beginning of Our Relationship	Synergy Level After We Did Our Healing Work
Expressing our anger together in a responsible way	In disagreement	In agreement
Expressing our joy together	In disagreement	Accept/honor
Expressing our sadness together in a responsible way	In disagreement	In agreement
Expressing our shame together in a responsible way	In agreement	In agreement
Expressing our love together	Accept/honor	Accept/honor
Expressing our fear together in a responsible way	In disagreement	In agreement
Expressing our excitement	In disagreement	Accept/honor
Channeling our anger together in a constructive way	In disagreement	Accept/honor
Channeling our joy together in a constructive way	In disagreement	Accept/honor
Channeling sadness together in a constructive way	Accept/honor	Accept/honor

Areas of the Heart/Emotions	Synergy Level at the Beginning of Our Relationship	Synergy Level After We Did Our Healing Work
Channeling shame together in a constructive way	Accept/honor	Accept/hono
Channeling love together in a constructive way	Accept/honor	Accept/honor
Channeling fear together in a constructive way	In disagreement	Accept/honor
Channeling excitement together in a constructive way	In disagreement	Accept/honor
Listening to each other's anger	In disagreement	Accept/honor
Listening to each other's joy	In disagreement	Accept/honor
Listening to each other's sadness	In agreement	In agreement
Listening to each other's shame	Accept/honor	In agreement
Listening to each other's love	In agreement	In agreement
Listening to each other's fear	Accept/honor	In agreement
Listening to each other's excitement	In disagreement	Accept/honor

As we mentioned earlier on in this chapter, the different ways to express an emotion are linked together. For example, if you have difficulty feeling anger, you won't be able to express it responsibly. Similarly, you will most certainly have trouble listening to your partner express anger and you will definitely not be able to channel it. The abilities to feel, to express, to listen to and to channel a specific emotion are linked together in a continuum. They operate together and influence each other. For this reason, we will review our own experience of each emotion through the full spectrum: feeling, expressing, channeling and listening to.

Anger: Feeling, Expressing, Listening to and Channeling

Ron and I had very different levels of ability with anger. As illustrated, I could easily feel my anger, whereas Ron had difficulty feeling his in the present moment. I could express my anger responsibly, Ron's anger came out sideways. When I listened to Ron expressing his anger, I often tried to fix it. He in turn reacted to my anger by getting angry himself. And as for channeling our anger together in a constructive way ... well, let's just say that it didn't happen!

We realized early on in our relationship that we had had totally different childhood models for anger. Ron never watched his parents express anger directly. Anger was a forbidden emotion in his family, one that he had not observed in others and that he didn't know how to experience in himself. As for me, I had often observed my father express his anger. Anger was familiar territory. As a teenager and as a young mother, I had expressed my own anger in irresponsible ways. For example, I sometimes screamed at my young son. One day, I watched him mimic my reactions and I understood in that moment that I had to get a handle on my own anger. Kids are a wonderful mirror for our shortcomings. I decided to learn to contain my anger and to express it in a responsible way. In fact, my children trained me in how to use my anger. The love that I felt for them motivated me to learn to master my anger.

When we first got together, Ron experienced anger in the following way. When I said something like, "I don't share your opinion about so and so," he felt anger and repressed it. His energy would go down. Later on in the conversation, he would get upset with me because I asked him a question. He would say, "Why are you asking this question? Haven't you been listening to what I just said?" I would become totally confused. Why would he get angry at me for asking a question? As I probed him, trying to find out what was wrong, he would shut down even more.

Mr. Meanie shows up. Whenever this cycle occurred, Ron's personality totally changed. He would become snappy and short. We called that part of him Mr. Meanie. Sometimes Mr. Meanie was in charge for days. Ron would be angry and aloof with me without knowing why. I, in turn, cringed and rejected his behaviors. I disagreed with how he expressed his anger. I had a lot of judgments about his Mr. Meanie. I thought that he was cruel and intentionally hurtful and took it personally. Even though I recognized that Ron had an issue with feeling and expressing anger, I still believed that he was out to get me.

I also had an issue with anger. I had trouble listening to Ron's anger without trying to fix him. I experienced a great deal of sadness when his Mr. Meanie showed up, convinced that he was trying to hurt me, I tried to change him. We had a cycle going on. When Mr. Meanie showed up, my Mrs. Fix-It would show up. Do you have any of those patterns in your relationship?

Moving out of the cycle. This cycle changed gradually. Ron's Mr. Meanie doesn't show up as much and when he does, the level of snappiness is way down. What enabled us to improve this area of our relationship was our willingness to take responsibility for our own experience and to allow the other his or her own experience. We were also both committed to speaking the truth about our experience and to owning that experience. Every time Ron's Mr. Meanie showed up, I shared how that felt for me in my body and in my heart; I talked about the sadness that I felt and about the tightness that I experienced in my body. I showed Ron my tears. I was willing to be vulnerable.

Ron improved his ability to recognize his anger when it showed up. He learned to manage its expression and to share his experience of anger instead of acting out in anger. For example, instead of snapping back at me when I asked him a question, he would tell me that he felt anger and that he wanted to snap at me.

I also improved my ability to simply listen to his expression of anger without trying to fix him. This was very difficult for me. In my profession as a management consultant I was used to clients asking for advice. They hired me for my counsel. So now I had to learn to simply listen without offering any advice.

Ron and I have come a long way in how we manage anger together. But there is more to do. Ron still has trouble tagging some of the anger that he feels. He doesn't always know where or why his anger is showing up, but he can now feel it in the present moment! I am still affected by how he expresses his anger, but I can now listen without giving advice!

The more we are willing to own our experience and share it, the deeper our level of intimacy. We discover hidden parts of ourselves under the pain. Ron has learned that much of his power is hidden under repressed anger and that by releasing it he can access his greater potential. I have experienced how deeply hurt I was as a child by uncontrolled expressions of anger and by negative comments about me. In doing my own healing work, I have also discovered hidden aspects of my sensitivity. I am more compassionate and sensitive with myself and others because of my experience of that childhood pain.

We accept and honor each other's level of ability at channeling anger. It is much easier for me to channel my anger than it is for Ron. I can experience anger, let it move through my body and then use the energy to do something constructive. For example, when I started writing this book, I experienced a great deal of resistance in the form of anger. I allowed myself to feel it. I allowed the emotion to move through my body. I discovered that I was holding on to a lot of anger from my childhood related to expressing my ideas. I remembered not being listened to when I tried to express my ideas. I remembered being made fun of when I shared a "different" perspective on certain issues. My anger was tremendous. I allowed it to move through my body and I used that energy to write this book. Because Ron and I are not at the same level of ability in channeling anger, it is hard for us to do so together. That is our next goal and our next step to increase our synergy in the area of anger.

Joy: Feeling, Expressing, Listening to and Channeling

Have you seen the movie "My Big Fat Greek Wedding"? In this love story about a Greek woman who falls in love with a typical white Anglo-Saxon man, the differences between their two cultures generate the funniest scenes of the movie. If you replace the word "Greek" with the word "French," the movie pretty much sums up Ron's and my cultural backgrounds. In my family, we love to laugh and we laugh with gusto. We love to tease each other. Teasing is never meant to hurt; it is a manifestation of love. In our culture, when you are laughing at someone you are giving them attention and showing them you care. Ron's family is much more subdued, like in the movie. Outward and boisterous displays of joy are not a common occurrence.

When Ron first visited my family in Montreal, he was in shock. We laughed a lot, talked all at the same time, teased each other. We loved to sit around the table and talk for hours. We drank wine and enjoyed food. We're Quebecers! French North Americans! He was overwhelmed by our ability to enjoy life. Feeling, expressing, listening to and channeling joy is easy for me. I was surrounded by joy in my culture. Even though my family life was not always joyous, I watched adults laughing, singing and having a wonderful time during family gatherings. I heard my parents and their friends roar with laughter during informal get-togethers or at some of the more lavished parties that they organized. I watched them dance and play games.

Ron tends to be more serious than I am. I love to play and tease. He is more somber. At the onset of our relationship, I was surprised at how little joy he experienced in his life. It was as if he didn't know how to feel joy or didn't quite know where or how to find joy in his being. My Mrs. Fix-It came to the rescue. I embarked on a crusade, the "crusade of the joyous." I tried to teach Ron how to be more joyous. I gave him numerous speeches on the merit of cultivating joy in his life. I must have been a royal pain. I had a lot of judgments about his difficulty at feeling and at expressing joy.

And, of course, I took it personally. My mind was besieged by the following thoughts: "If he isn't joyous, I must be doing something wrong." " I am not making him happy." " Marriage is supposed to be fun … isn't it?" Ron's issues with creating joy in his life brought some of my own childhood wounds to the surface. I remembered my mother's depression and my attempts at making her feel better. It had been excruciatingly painful for me to experience her somber moods, to feel the tension in her being.

As a married partner, it was just as painful for me to live with a man who felt and expressed little joy. I experienced my joy being dragged down and my mood becoming more somber when Ron didn't respond in kind to my joy, just as I had experienced with my mother. I shared those wounds with Ron. I allowed my little girl inside to express her need and her want for joy. I allowed the tears to show up. Gradually, I allowed myself to experience joy with or without Ron. I discovered the pleasures of laughing by myself even when the other person in the room is experiencing little or no joy. I learned that I can feel joy even if it is not reciprocated by my partner. I accepted and honored that Ron was unable to share that experience with me as much as we both would like him to.

Ron's ability to feel and to express joy has greatly improved. He is learning to tap into his joyous inner little boy and is becoming more playful. As children, we emulate our parents' behaviors and attitudes towards life. If we were surrounded by serious adults, very likely we will become serious ourselves. It takes a great deal of courage and determination to create new emotional patterns. Ron has recognized his need for joy. He wants to feel and express more joy in his life. He has experienced the impact of it on his body and on his mind. He knows that when he is joyful, his body is more relaxed and his mind is more peaceful. Until he is able to generate joy freely from within himself, it remains difficult for him to channel joy energy into constructive endeavors.

We have increased our synergy level in terms of expressing and listening to each other's joy. We are now able to channel joy together to pursue our dreams!!!

Sadness: Feeling, Expressing, Listening to and Channeling

Ron was a revelation to me in terms of sadness. He could name his sadness, totally surrender to the feeling of it, ask to be held, cry and simply let the emotion move through him. He was a master at experiencing sadness in all its forms. To this day, I have never met

I'm Right...You Need to Change

another man who allows himself to feel and express sadness the way Ron does. Unfortunately, for most men, displays of sadness are a sign of weakness. A man should be strong at all times. This is still a sign of our times. Ron learned to honor his sadness early on in his life.

Considering the fact that I didn't know how to cry in front of anyone, his mastery with sadness was good for me. I remember the first few times that I shared sadness with Ron. I told him, "I feel sad." He asked if I wanted to be held. I said, "Yes, that would be nice." After a few minutes, he asked me if I was feeling my sadness and I responded, "Yes, I am." Then he asked me where my tears where.

The inner gutters. I started looking for my tears. I had none on the outside, but they were pouring within me. Instead of allowing my tears to flow freely from my eyes, I had developed inner gutters. My tears flowed inside of me. I recalled that my mother never allowed herself to cry. To this day, she refuses to cry. Because of her inability to feel and to express her own sadness, she never created a safe space for me to express mine. I learned early on that showing my tears was not an option. It would create pain for my mother or so I thought at the time. I could feel my sadness, cry by myself and I could listen to someone else's sadness. But, I couldn't cry in front of anyone.

It took me a while to allow my tears to come out. After all, I had major reconstruction to do, building outside gutters and taking out the inner ones. I remember the incredible feeling of vulnerability that I experienced the first few times I allowed myself to cry in Ron's arms. Due to my early experiences, part of me was convinced that he would reject the expression of my sadness. Ron's incredible mastery with sadness allowed me to heal that area of my life. I can now cry when I need to. I feel safe and totally validated in my experience of sadness. Our ability to feel, to express and to listen to sadness nurtures our relationship. We both know that we can share our pain with each other and that our partner honors our experience of sadness.

Having mastered the feeling, expression and listening to sadness, we are now able to channel the energy contained in that emotion. For example, if we experience sadness about a specific situation such as the war in Iraq, we can share it with each other and allow the emotion to move through our bodies. We can then use that energy to focus on specific actions. Those actions may be prayer and meditation or holding the thought of peace in our mind. The experience of creating synergy by channeling our sadness energy together increases the alignment of our couple in purpose and in deed. What an incredible experience of synergy!!!

Shame: Feeling, Expressing, Listening to and Channeling

Both Ron and I had done considerable work on our own shame before we became a couple. However, when you work out your shame issues with your friends or with a therapist, you don't achieve the depth of experience that you do in an intimate relationship, so there was still work to do.

Sexual intimacy in conjunction with emotional intimacy reveals deeper levels of shame. The more you open your heart and your body to love, the greater the opportunity to feel your shame. Even after years of therapy, workshops and classes, I still held a considerable amount of shame in my body. This shame was related to physical abuse I had endured as a child and was lodged deep within my sexual organs. Needless to say that the shame showed up when I opened up sexually to Ron.

Both Ron and I were able to feel, to express and to listen to each other's shame. However, I did not expect the level and depth of pain that was still locked into my body. I remember lying in bed for hours, re-experiencing shame from my childhood. As Ron held me, I cried and choked on my tears. My body shook between convulsions as it released childhood memories of abuse. After each healing episode, I was in an altered state of consciousness for the rest of the day, sometimes even for several days. My body was totally sensitive to every sensation, I could fall apart and cry if Ron spoke to me with a strong voice. I wanted to hide.

During those aftermaths, I experienced my body as if it was shedding its skin. That's how raw I felt. I experienced letting down my defense mechanisms and being as vulnerable as a child. I had rendered my inner child vulnerable to the outside world by allowing past memories to resurface. Wonderful energy was released deep from within my body following each one of these healings of my shame. I had freed up part of my inner child and that child was allowing its natural joy and love to surface.

These healing episodes lasted for a few months at the very beginning of our relationship. As Ron and I created a cycle of intimacy, time and time again, I revealed a deeper level of shame. As I did so, he responded with deeper levels of compassion. My being willing to share the depth of my shame opened his heart to more love. His willingness to embrace all of my shame enabled me to heal it. This healing cycle created a depth of synergy in our relationship.

At this point, shame does not show up in our relationship. That's because it doesn't show up much in each one of us any more. But when it does, we are able to feel it, express it and listen to it. We are also able to channel the energy contained in shame.

Love: Feeling, Expressing, Listening to and Channeling

Ron and I express love in different ways and with different levels of intensity. As in the case of joy, I express love with a lot more intensity than Ron does. I am generally more demonstrative than he is. Initially, I was disappointed with his ability to demonstrate affection. I wanted more hugs, more kisses and more intensity. In my mind, I equated intensity of demonstration of love with intensity of feeling. In other words, the more you love someone, the more you shower that person with kisses and hugs. Therefore, I reasoned, if Ron felt a great deal of love for me, he would demonstrate it often and with intensity.

Conversely, if he didn't shower me with affection, I decided that he couldn't possibly love me intensely. When I started to perceive the differences in how we expressed our love, I started withdrawing. I started doubting the intensity of his love for me and withheld my own demonstrations of love. I didn't touch him as much, I didn't kiss him as much and I didn't hug him as much.

The problem for me was that I was depriving myself of what I wanted. That is, by giving less affection, I was receiving less. Ron, on the other hand, didn't seem to be bothered by my restrictive expressions of affection. I was reacting like a child. I was pouting because I wasn't getting what I wanted. My inner process was very similar to what can be observed in children of 5 or 6 years old. "If you're not my friend, I won't be yours anymore." A child often responds to another child in that manner. Children learn to negotiate by asking for what they want and withdrawing if they don't get what they want. However, I was no longer a child. I had to take a hard look at my issues. I still had a child wound about not getting enough affection from my dad. As I had withdrawn from him, I was now withdrawing from my husband.

The adult in me quickly recognized that that did not work for me. I had to come up with a different strategy. I allowed myself to go for what I wanted. If I wanted a hug, I went to get it. If I wanted a kiss, I gave one. Within a matter of days, I noticed that I was feeling a lot more love and I was fulfilling my need for affection. I had empowered myself in meeting my emotional needs and wants. We were both able to feel, express and listen to love. But we did so within the confines of our childhood and cultural backgrounds. In my family we show our love often and with intensity. In Ron's family love is not often shown; it's as if the feeling is taken for granted and the demonstration of it is therefore not needed. I am now at peace with Ron's expression of love. I honor and accept that he has learned to express his love very differently than I have. On the other hand, Ron allows himself greater expression of his affection.

I take responsibility for getting what I want. Out of doing my inner healing work, I am now empowered to create the level of love that I want to experience. Ron and I can channel the energy from our love to create the vision that we hold for our life. The love we have for each other is channeled in the work we do with others. Our styles of expression may be very different; yet, our love is aligned with our mission in life and with our commitment to support each other in becoming the best that we can be.

Fear: Feeling, Expressing, Listening to and Channeling

As mentioned earlier, Ron and I had very different philosophies of life. His was more passive; he allowed events to unfold. Mine was more active; I believed in establishing a vision and goals for my life and doing whatever was necessary to actualize them. These differences in philosophy were also reflected in how we dealt with fear. We could both feel and express fear. In that we experienced synergy. However, I had a time limit for how long I could express fear. After feeling and expressing it, I believed I had to redirect the energy to follow a course of action.

This had worked well in my life. In my business, as in any business, we went through the ups and downs of the market. When the results were not meeting our expected financial projections, I experienced fear. Would I have to fire anyone? Would I have to cut expenses? What would happen to the business? After feeling that fear and looking at the causes, I would align with a course of action. What could I do? What marketing plan could my partners and I set in motion? In other words, I learned to use my fear and to channel its energy into constructive endeavors.

Ron, on the other hand, allowed his fear to simply be. He could stay in fear for days. He was practicing what he believed in, that is, letting things evolve at their own rhythm and in their own time. When we first started our business, there were a lot of uncertainties about how to market our services. Our income initially did not support our lifestyle. We had many opportunities to experience fear. I went through my usual process; I acknowledged my fear, experienced it and worked on finding solutions. Ron stayed in his fear for much longer.

I had no patience with his attitude. I had a lot of judgment about people who stayed in fear without doing anything to move to the next level. I had no respect for that kind of behavior. Not surprisingly, my Mrs. Fix-It showed up. I experienced a lot of anger for Ron. How could he stay in fear? Didn't he know how destructive that emotion was? Didn't he know that by staying in fear he wasn't helping our business? I tried to coach him. I attempted to prove to him how destructive fear was. I tried to support him in finding what the cause of his fear was. As could be expected, he resisted and closed off. I had no compassion. With my mind in charge, I knew we needed to move on and act

As in other areas of our life, Ron and I looked within for the answers to the separation we were experiencing. I acknowledged that I was acting with Ron in the same way that my dad had acted with me. I had never experienced any compassion from him for my fears and my doubts. I don't think that I was ever able to communicate any of those thoughts or those feelings to him. He wasn't open to that. I modeled my behavior on his.

Ron, for his part, had decided as a child that he could never do anything right, remembering the many times when what he attempted did not meet with his father's approval. He never seemed to do it right. Why should he try to change the course of his life? It was a foregone conclusion that all his attempts at creating the outcome he wanted would fail. He learned to do the same thing with his emotions. His belief that he would fail in creating the life that he wanted also included the belief that he could not master his own emotions. So he simply surrendered to them, allowing them to run their course without attempting to channel them to constructive ends.

By taking responsibility for our experience of fear and of each other, and by doing our inner work, we discovered hidden treasures in our being. I connected with a much deeper level of compassion for others and for myself. Ron discovered that he could make choices and that he could choose to channel the fear energy into something creative. I am now able to simply listen to Ron's fear. He, on the other hand, doesn't allow himself to delve in it without limit. We are learning to channel the energy released from fear into action. We can share and experience our fears and identify together the actions that we need to implement. Our synergy increases every time we honor each other's fear and then focus its energy to make a difference in our life.

Excitement: Feeling, Expressing, Listening to and Channeling

Joy, love and excitement are linked to our different backgrounds and cultures. Latin people are generally more expressive; they thrive on enjoying life. They are more easily excitable. If you have traveled in Italy and in France and then go to England or to Holland, you will immediately notice obvious differences. Don't talk to anyone, simply observe people on the streets. Notice the body language, the sound of the voices. Notice in France and in Italy, people use body gestures to express their emotions; they also speak louder. Then, notice in Britain and in Holland, people appear calm and collected when they express themselves. The differences are obvious.

Ron and I experienced excitement in very different ways. I kept finding opportunities for celebration. I enjoy the simple details of life. I love sharing that excitement. Ron didn't seem to get excited about anything. His experience was more even keeled than mine.

Gradually, Ron has recognized that the more he celebrates life, the more he gets out of his experience of it. To this day, he is still developing his ability to find excitement in the simple things of life.

Chapter 6

Your Bodies Working Together
The Path of the Body

What Is the Path of the body?

We have two types of experiences with our bodies. In the inner experience, we feel sensations such as pain and pleasure. In the outer experience, we organize resources in our environment such as money or the furniture in our house. What links these two experiences is our ability to act. For example, if you experience pleasure when eating certain foods, you will seek out those same foods to repeat the experience. You will act to increase the pleasurable sensations in your body. In the same vein, if you need more money in order to pay your bills, you may look for new employment opportunities or take on a second job. You will act to organize the resources in your life.

Feeling sensations, organizing resources and acting are the three attributes of the path of the body.

Sensations

Your sensations enable you to know what is going on in your body. When you feel pain, pleasure, tightness and varying levels of energy, for example, you can process these sensations to get information. You look for answers to questions such as, What is the source of my pain? What gives me pleasure? Why is my energy so low? You can act on the information provided by your sensations.

Sensations within your body may reflect the state of other dimensions of your being. For instance, tightness in your chest may reflect the fear that you are experiencing in a specific situation. If you have negative thoughts, you may feel tense and if you are having loving thoughts about someone, you may have a feeling of warmth. Your body sensations often reflect what is going on in your mind, in your heart and in your will.

The body never lies. If you are able and willing to listen, it will let you know what is going on in the other dimensions of your being. The ability to discern the source of sensations in your body is a powerful skill on the journey down the path of the body. By becoming more conscious of your experience, you increase your ability to create the experience you want. Consciousness is the first step to freedom of action.

With your senses you also experience the outside environment. With your sight you can enjoy art. With a glance you can communicate love. With your sense of smell you can experience the wonderful fragrance of wild flowers or the delicate scent of fine perfume. With your sense of taste you can savor the flavors of different foods. With your sense of hearing you can enjoy music or hear your children laughing. With your sense of touch you can feel your partner's skin and experience the textures of different objects.

Sharing these experiences with your partner increases your physical intimacy. Whether you are sharing the sensations within your body or your experiences of the environment around you, you are opening up to your partner. Together, you uncover the mysteries of your bodies.

Action and Resources

The body enables you to act in the world. Without a body, you can't actualize your dreams and vision in the physical universe. You act your love by hugging your children. You follow your dreams by building a home. You reach a goal by saving money.

The ability to organize resources is key in reaching your dreams. The challenge lies in finding systems (ways of organizing) that both partners can support. For instance, if you can devise a systematic and common way to save money, you are paving the way to shared financial wealth. If you can identify a common approach and guidelines to raising your children, you will increase your joy of parenting together. It takes systems to manage resources together successfully. Being able to do so dramatically increases your level of synergy together.

There are many opportunities to create synergy with your partner on the path of the body. These opportunities exist within the areas listed below. We discuss each one in the pages that follow.
- Day-to-day living
- Participation in the community
- Entertainment, extracurricular activities
- Financial: how you manage money

- Children: how you raise children
- Sexuality
- Expressing affection physically
- Sleeping habits
- Playing: having fun, joking, teasing, playing roles, inventing games, etc.)
- Vacation (locations, number of trips and duration)
- Food: quantity and quality
- Work: the importance of work in life
- Car (taking care of it and driving it)
- Your body (taking care of it, working out)
- How you implement decisions (doing what it takes to make things happen after a decision is made)
- Feeling sensations in your body

The Areas of Synergy in Your Relationship

Day-to-Day-Living

How do you experience day-to-day living with your partner? Is it easy and fun to do housework together or is it a constant struggle? Do you have similar views and habits with regard to how housecleaning is done or is one of you "cleaner" than the other. These issues must be addressed early on if you want to avoid living in a constant state of frustration and turmoil.

You won't be able to change your partner. Take a hard look at how you both behave in this area. Don't believe for one minute that you can "make" your partner into your ideal version of a housekeeper. Accept what is. Acknowledge what your needs and wants are in terms of housekeeping. Go through your house. What do you need or want in the bathroom? What do you need or want in your bedroom? Be honest and frank with your partner. Write your needs and wants on a list and identify your "must haves" and your "nice to haves." "Must haves" are things that you don't want to give up. "Nice to haves" are things that you would like to have but that you are willing to give up.

Also, identify in your home the common living spaces and some private areas for each partner. Decide together how the common spaces will be maintained taking into account each partner's "nice to haves" and the "must haves." Who will do what, when? Agree on specific responsibilities and timeframe for chores. Allow each partner to manage the private areas assigned to each in his or her own way.

The space that you live in should be a comfortable and warm nesting area for your relationship. If you live in harmony on a day-to day basis, you'll be able to create a safe and nurturing home. Your home is the physical center of your lives. It is the place where you can go for rejuvenation. It is your sacred grounding space. For this reason it is important that both partners find in the home a reflection of their individual needs and wants as well as an expression of their ability to create synergy together by managing housekeeping in a harmonious way.

I'm Right...You Need to Change

Participation in the Community

Your family unit is part of a greater community. Your relationship with the community may either be limited or extensive. By sharing a similar level of participation with your partner, you create common interests. You also increase your experience of belonging together. For example, you share friends as you go about volunteering at your church or in a hospital.

Participation in the community together increases your sense of identity as a couple. That is, people acknowledge you for your partnership; they can provide you with encouragement and assistance in times of trouble. The community serves as an anchor for your family unit and as such supports the synergy of your relationship.

Entertainment, Extracurricular Activities

What type of entertainment do you and your partner prefer? Do you enjoy going to the movies together, having guests for dinner or playing card games? Or do you have very different entertainment interests and activities? The more activities you share, the greater your experience of synergy together. Find some common activities that you both enjoy and set specific times to do them.

How You Manage Money

Chapter 4 includes a section on the importance of having a vision, goals and a plan with your partner. This includes having financial goals together. These goals drive how you manage money. Take the time to discuss these goals together, and make a plan and follow it.

Coming up with a system to manage your money is impossible unless you first decide on your goals. How much will you save and how often? What is your budget for recurring expenses? What about entertainment? If you have no idea what goals you are pursuing and have not reached an agreement on those goals, it is difficult to implement a budget. Some of our clients disagree on what the expenses should be. When they decide what their goals are, based on their needs and their wants, managing expenses becomes part of managing their wealth together.

Once a general budget has been agree upon, it is also important to clarify the roles and responsibilities of budgeting, paying the bills and the general management of finances. Will you share the responsibility of managing the budget or will one partner take on that task? Make sure that you are both comfortable with your respective roles and that you support each other in those roles. Most issues related to how we manage money stem from a lack of planning or poor financial management. Having clear goals and a plan aligned with your vision as a couple as well as specific roles and responsibilities will enable you to create synergy in this area of your relationship.

How You Raise Children

Many parents disagree on how to raise their children. We often discover with our clients that they are raising their children the way they would have wanted to be raised themselves. In other words, they are compensating for their own unresolved childhood needs. In such cases, the real "objective" needs of the children have not been clearly defined or discussed by both partners. Instead, the childhood needs of one or of both parents have been projected onto the child. Let's illustrate this with an example.

A woman was terrified by her father who abused her physically and emotionally. When she had a child of her own, a daughter, she tried to protect her from her partner's anger. For example, she would interfere when her partner tried to discipline the child, holding discipline as abuse. Unconsciously, she was trying to heal her own childhood wound by protecting her daughter. She was still carrying fear and possibly terror from her own experiences as a child and projected that terror on her daughter. She couldn't discern real and appropriate anger from emotional abuse.

Raising children is a wonderful opportunity to revisit your childhood wounds as long as you don't project those wounds on your children! In the example above, the mother may notice that she cringes when her husband gets angry at their daughter. She can then contain her experience of fear and discern whether the husband's anger is appropriate given the circumstances or whether there is real emotional and/or physical abuse. Recognizing her own wound and separating her own experience of abuse from the reality of the present moment will enable her to let go of her past by not interfering in the relationship between daughter and father. She may later choose to share her experience with her partner and do her own healing work by reliving and releasing her own childhood traumas.

Addressing your children's needs. How your raise your children should be defined by their real needs, not by what you believe them to be from the perspective of your own wounded childhood.

Children have emotional needs. They need to be loved and they also need to have their experience validated. Confirming with them what they are feeling is a great way to do this. For example, when your child is angry, you may say, "You are really angry about that, aren't you?" Letting children express their anger reinforces their experience that it is okay to be angry. At the same time, children must be shown how to manage their emotions. For example, with anger you may tell your child, "I see that you are angry and that's okay. You have every right to feel angry, but it's not appropriate to hit your sister. You can speak your anger but you can't act it out." Modeling is an important part of parenting. If your children watch you express your anger responsibly, they will learn that emotions are okay and they will learn how to express them responsibly.

Children's minds also have needs. Helping them discern the difference between fact and judgment at a young age will support them in developing the ability to understand the world in an objective way. Validate their judgments as you help them identify the facts specific to a given situation. Supporting your children in making decisions based on facts and not on judgments will serve them well in their professional as well as in their personal life.

The more you expose your children to different cultures and different experiences, the more aware they become of the diversity of life and its vast possibilities. It will be easier for them to imagine living an exciting and original life. Encouraging them to have dreams and to figure out how to make them happen will also empower them in being able to create a successful life for themselves.

In the dimension of the body, kids obviously need good food and sufficient rest. They also should be encouraged to discover ways to exercise their bodies. If they express passion for a specific sport or activity; encourage it. A lifestyle is taken on early in life. Support your children in developing one that will generate and maintain health later on.

Invite your children to share what they experience in their bodies. Validate their aches and pains; ask them what they are feeling. Decide on a wide range of experiences of the senses. Trying different foods when they are young broadens their eating experience and habits. Invite all of their comments and ideas; help them discover what works for their bodies.

On a spiritual level, encourage your children to talk about their understanding of God or any other higher being. Pick a church, a spiritual group or other source of spiritual teachings that empower your child's sense of responsibility and of creativity. Support them in discovering a relationship with their inner source. It will serve them for the rest of their lives.

These are but a few examples of your children's needs. Take the time to discuss them with your partner, and agree on behaviors to be modeled in front of the children and on your standards for discipline. Agree to never disagree about how you raise children in front of them. If you have any disagreements, discuss them in private. If you don't demonstrate a common approach in front of the children, they will quickly learn to play you against each other.

Raising children is a wonderful opportunity to strengthen your relationship with your partner. However, synergy will only emerge if both partners can differentiate between what the children really need and what they are attempting to heal within themselves, and if there is a common agreement on the rules and the accepted behaviors.

Sexuality

Sexual intimacy stems from emotional intimacy. This is especially true for women. In their initial coaching sessions, couples often confide that they have issues with sexual intimacy. As they go about resolving other issues and learn to develop new ways to bond emotionally, their sexual issues usually dissolve.

In order for a woman to open her body and receive her partner's love, she has to open her heart. When resentment, anger, shame and fear are present between partners, the heart cannot open. There is no room for love. We observe this in how a woman holds her body. The messages are clear we perceive tightness in the shoulders and in the chest, the body is closed because the heart is closed. Take care of your heart, share your feelings, let go of resentment and learn to keep your emotional energy moving. Sexual openness will follow.

Certain physical conditions such as hormonal imbalance may explain dysfunctional sexual symptoms. These can usually be taken care of through proper medical attention. However, if this is not the case, check how you feel in your heart about your partner. Check the thoughts you have about your partner. If you can communicate and let go of negative feelings and negative thoughts, your sexual energy will start to flow.

If your sexual practices are not satisfying and you long for something different or more nurturing, have a frank and honest discussion about your needs and wants with your partner. You may not be very good at asking for what you want. Isn't it sad to find out that you could have gotten what you wanted 10 or 12 years ago. All you had to do was ask.

If you are shy or uncomfortable about discussing your sexual needs and wants with your partner, go within and look at your feelings. Do you believe that you shouldn't need to ask? Do you believe that your needs and wants are not important? Are you embarrassed by what you need and want? If so, where did you learn that? Why do you have such beliefs or thoughts? Share this with your partner and choose to live outside of your box and ask for what you want. It has been our experience that most partners are more than willing to satisfy their partner's sexual wants and needs especially if theirs are also met. Take a chance; you have nothing to lose and all to gain in terms of increased synergy.

Expressing Affection Physically

Expressing affection physically is also a function of how open your heart is. The comments mentioned under sexuality apply to the expression of affection. If you are not experiencing love for your partner but are hanging on to resentment, anger or fear, your body is tense and closed. A closed body does not naturally reach out to touch another. Healing your heart by releasing negative emotions and discussing openly your needs for affection will empower you in creating the type and quality of affectionate behavior that you desire.

Sleeping Habits

The body needs to rest at night, and so does your relationship. Sleeping quietly, cuddling and snuggling together heals the body, mind and heart and helps rebuild your stamina for the day. You are not only giving each other physical warmth and comfort, you are also creating joy and love for the heart as well as loving images for the mind.

Some people have trouble enjoying a deep and nurturing sleep. If that's the case, check your diet, your intake of caffeine, the amount of sugar you ingest, the level of stress in your job. Find appropriate expertise to ensure that your nights are quiet and rejuvenating. And enjoy them with your partner. Mornings with your partner are different after a night of cuddling and snuggling.

Playing together: Having Fun, Joking, Teasing, etc.

Most of us take ourselves way too seriously. We have stressful jobs and innumerable responsibilities. We become "real" adults. We probably watched our parents being "serious" adults. We may have taken on the belief that when you are an adult, you must behave seriously.

Learn to play again; rediscover your joyous inner child. As you do your healing work by owning your emotions and linking them to your childhood wounds, your mischievous playful child starts to emerge. When you can play with your partner, you create joy and release stress. You are creating the best possible form of synergy. When you become child-like, you relax, you learn that it is okay to be a bit goofy, to be ridiculous, outrageous. Playfulness gives space for creativity and for the spontaneous expression of healthy craziness. When you can play with you partner, you are building a reservoir of love and joy to help you through times of stress and conflict.

If you are having trouble being playful with your partner, you are either holding on to resentment or you have not allowed your inner child to surface. Check your feelings for your partner. Do you hold your partner in a loving way in your mind? If you're hanging on to a past incident or to anger, share it and let it go. If, on the other hand, you have never experienced your joyful inner child, call him/her forth. Choose to get back in touch with yourself when you were between 3 and 7 years old. Watch small children; look at how they play. You may have to do some inner healing work. Our joyous child usually doesn't show up if there is a sad or angry inner child waiting to be validated. To access the joyous child within you, you need to take care of the wounded inner child first. The more you are willing to heal your inner wounds, the more joy you can access. You have playfulness within you, bring it out and then share that with your partner.

Vacation (Locations, Number of Trips and Duration)

Enjoying your vacations together is a reflection of your ability to enjoy life together. Anything that is not resolved or not working in your relationship tends to show up during your vacations. To enjoy great vacations, take care of your relationship on a daily basis.

You and your partner may have different interests, wants and needs when it comes to vacations. You may want a vacation close to the ocean, whereas your partner may want to visit museums and listen to concerts. Establish what your needs and wants are, then find a vacation plan that meets all your needs, and don't forget the relationship. Remember, the relationship is a third entity that also has needs. During your vacation, keep your relationship playful. Clear disagreements; let go of negative feelings. Have fun!

When was the last time you went on vacation with your partner? What a great way to reconnect and to create new memories to enhance your synergy together.

Food (Quantity and Quality)

What a pleasure it is to enjoy with your partner the aromas and flavors of a carefully crafted meal. You may not often take the time to appreciate the foods that you ingest. We tend to rush through life, following heavy schedules that leave little time to appreciate meals.

Spend time with your partner talking about the foods you enjoy. Learn to cook together, commit yourselves to discovering different foods. Make one or two special meals a week, possibly with a good bottle of wine, some candles and the right music to create a romantic atmosphere.

Make sure you are open with each other. Eating and being in a state of anger, resentment or fear don't go well together. Clear the air if necessary. Then, take the time to enjoy each bite, each aroma. As you learn to relax and enjoy your food, mealtimes become another opportunity to get closer to your partner and to create a family experience. They say that the way to a man's heart is through his stomach. That works for women also!

Managing The Importance of Work in Life

Much of our time is spent at work. Further, the time dedicated to our work often exceeds the time actually spent at work. That is, our physical bodies may be at home but our minds are still at the office. It is easy to tilt the balance of time in your life in favor of work.

Leading a balanced life is essential to the success of your relationship. Many couples have lifestyle issues. They find it next to impossible to spend quality time with their partner. They may have become workaholics because they did not have the skills to create real intimacy with their partner.

Most people don't know how to communicate their feelings; they don't have the ability to manage conflicts and discussions in a positive way, and they have forgotten how to play and enjoy themselves. If you are spending more time at work than you know you should, if work has become the main focus of your life, if you know in your heart that you crave more time with your partner but haven't been able to make it happen, look at yourself. Notice what you think of yourself when you envision spending more time with your partner. Do you see yourself as successful at doing that or do you question your ability to create true intimacy?

Notice what you feel in your heart when you consider spending time with your partner. Do you have fear in your heart that it won't work out or are you excited about the possibility? Share these thoughts and emotions with your partner. Talk about the reasons why you have allowed your work to take precedence over your relationship. Go beyond the logistics of creating balance in your life to the underlying reasons for not having done so. Share the discomfort you may be feeling when attempting to create intimacy.

I'm Right...You Need to Change

You may be avoiding certain issues; discuss these issues with your partner. Find out why you have not created that special time with your partner.

Only when you are willing to be totally honest and vulnerable with each other and to talk about the real motivations behind your problems will you be able to make strides in resolving your lifestyle issues. Balance in your life will flow naturally from your increased awareness, and planning time together will no longer be a struggle. Remember, your relationship requires the commitment of your time. The level of priority of work in your life needs to be aligned with your relationship goals.

Car (Taking Care of It and Driving It)

This is seldom a major issue in a relationship. If you have issues over taking care of your car, it may be sufficient to clarify the roles and responsibilities of each partner. By agreeing on this or by simply confirming what is tacitly agreed upon, issues can usually easily be resolved.

Taking Care of Your Body

Taking care of our body and staying healthy is an individual responsibility. It is not one that can be shared. How we take care of our body is often a reflection of our level of self-esteem. Each partner needs to be responsible for his/her own body by choosing the right nutritional exercise/sport program.

If you have concerns about your partner's health, communicate and discuss them honestly and openly. Ultimately, the responsibility for choosing a proper course of action and for acting on that course remains with the individual. If you don't like the appearance of your partner (weight, hair color, etc.), look inside and determine what your real concerns are about. If they are not health related but considerations about image, it is a sure sign that you need to do some kind of transformational healing work.

Notice how you feel about your partner's appearance and how you feel about how he or she takes care of the body? What are your judgments? Scrutinize your thoughts and feelings around that subject. Verify whether your concerns are based on facts related to health (being overweight stresses the heart and can endanger health) or on an inner rigid image of beauty (thin women are more attractive) and do your own healing work. Look inside to discover what your true motivation is. Is it really about your partner, or is it more that you feel better about yourself if he or she looks a certain way? Imagine walking down the street with your partner. Are you ashamed of what people will say about you if they see your partner, or are you simply ashamed of what they will say about your partner?

Some of our clients are adamant that their partners have a particular physical appearance. They often discover during the course of a session that these concerns hide some deep inner shame within themselves. You may look for beauty in someone else and come up with a rigid definition of that beauty because you fail to see beauty within yourself. Individuals who possess an integrated experience of their own inner beauty along with compassion for their own shortcomings tend to be more flexible in what they expect from their partners.

Creating synergy with your partner in this area is about accepting/honoring how your partner takes care of his/her body. You may even want to share with your partner a particular diet and/or some type of training or exercise regime. As with all other areas, the more you share together, the more you increase your synergy. However, different bodies have different needs in terms of nutrition and health maintenance. Accepting and honoring each other in the choices that each partner makes will increase the joy, compassion and love that you feel for each other.

How You Implement Decisions

Great ideas are not always acted upon. How many great ideas have you dropped before you even tried to make them happen? You and your partner may have different levels of ability when it comes to implementing decisions. If decisions do not affect the synergy between partners, the fact that partners have different levels of ability in implementing decisions need not impact the relationship. For instance, you decide to play racquetball with friends twice a week. After a month, you notice that you haven't followed through with that decision. The fact that you didn't implement the decision does not affect your relationship it was an individual decision. It is not up to your partner to question why you didn't act on your decision. It is up to you to look inside to find out the truth about your lack of follow-through.

However, if a decision is made conjointly and if clear and precise tasks have been assigned to each person, failure to act on the decisions made and on the tasks chosen becomes an issue for the couple. For instance, you decide that both of you will deposit a specific amount each week in a vacation account at your bank. After two months, you notice that your partner has not deposited his or her share of the money. In this case, both partners are impacted by one partner's failure to follow through on the decision. When that happens, sit down and discuss the situation. Revisit your commitment. Are you still committed to the decision you made? If you're not, make a decision that you can both support. Revisit your plan. Did you plan the appropriate activities to guarantee successful implementation of your decision? If not, change them and make a new commitment to the new plan or confirm your commitment to the original plan. Define what kind of support you need from each other to enact your plan. Identify how you will follow through on the plan that you designed together. Most important, let go of the past, forgive and forget your own as well as your partner's shortcomings. Start afresh and learn from the experience.

You improve your skills in a particular area if you are able to recognize the facts about what did not work and if you are willing to learn the lessons embedded in your own shortcomings. Why do you have trouble implementing decisions? Where did you learn that? Is it a common or a rare occurrence? What excuses do you come up with when it happens? When you don't follow through on your decisions, you are weakening your will as well as your self-esteem. If the decision was made with your partner, you are also decreasing the level of synergy of your relationship. Find out the cause behind your difficulty with following through. Look into your childhood; that is where your will was nurtured or thwarted. When you find the specific childhood experiences or wounds behind your issues with following through, give yourself time to heal. For example, one of our clients was constantly reprimanded when he completed a chore. He could never meet his parents' standards of excellence.

Early on, he concluded that no matter what he did, they would never be satisfied. As an adult, he avoided making decisions or following through on the few decisions that he did make. He had a deeply ingrained belief that no matter how hard he tried, he could never be successful. What is the cause of your issues with making decisions or with following through? Share your healing journey with your partner.

Implementing decisions together is a wonderful opportunity to strengthen your relationship. You are left with a sense of power. You can reach goals and act in synergy together!

Feeling Sensations in Your Body

Each of us has different levels of awareness of our bodies. Some of us feel very little in our bodies; others feel a great deal. Ron and I do a lot of work with our clients around bringing consciousness into the body. We ask people to describe what they feel at a specific moment in every part of their body. The answers we get vary from "I don't feel anything" or "I feel numb," to a precise and detailed description of every sensation in every part of the body. Why such differences?

Differences stem from two different sources. First, as part of our genetic make-up, we are born with different levels of sensitivity. This is apparent already in children. For example, some children are more sensitive to pain than others. Some children like to be touched and caressed more than others. The other source of differences in degree of physical sensitivity between individuals resides in how open our bodies are. When partners come to us for coaching, they have often shut down their bodies' sensitivity by holding on to negative emotions. The intimacy of their relationship has reactivated childhood wounds that they were previously unable to recognize as such and release. Closing their bodies enabled them to avoid the pain.

For example, if you were physically abused as a child, you probably learned to cut yourself off from that experience. The pain of being hit time and time again was devastating. To deal with it, you shut down your nervous system and generated numbness throughout your body. Now, move forward 20 years. If you are not conscious of what you did to your body during those years of abuse, it is probably still shut down.

Repressed childhood trauma is a root cause of a lot of the tightness and stress people experience in their bodies. They may have tense muscles or suffer from rigidity in their limbs. When they start opening their bodies up and willingly re-experience the pain repressed there, they often experience intense physical rejuvenation. During one of our coaching sessions a man was able to relive the pain that he experienced when abused by his father. He released the fear and the sadness from his body. The following week he started noticing pain and pleasure in his body. Previously, he had cut himself off from his ability to feel.

You were born with the ability to feel sensations in your body. As a child, you most certainly experienced some type of emotional or physical pain that you encapsulated in your body. That part of your body closed off and became numb. It is up to you to free up your body or keep it shut down. You have the choice to allow your body to reach its full potential level of sensitivity. The willingness of each partner to open his or her body and to feel contributes greatly to intimacy. Intimacy exists in all forms, not only as sensual and sexual intimacy, but also as emotional intimacy. If your body is closed off to the pain that you incurred as a child through physical abuse, for example, you have not only repressed that pain but also any feeling of joy and love that you can experience when your partner touches you.

Shut down from your own physical sensations (tightness in the abdomen, for example), you are unable to receive the energy and love emanating from your partner's hands. Intimacy starts with the heart, but it goes through the body. The heart and the body are closely tied together. They are already working in synergy. If your body is holding on to pain from childhood, your heart cannot generate love to transform the pain into joy. Opening your body to repressed sensations and emotions is essential in creating intimacy. Once you have released pent-up energy from past childhood wounds, you are free to enjoy the pleasure of your partner's caresses.

YOUR SYNERGY CHECKLIST
REMEMBER:

You can increase your synergy on the path of the body if you:
- Enjoy day-to-day living in your home together
- Participate together in community activities
- Enjoy entertainment activities together
- Manage money efficiently together
- Raise children in harmony with each other
- Enjoy a rich sexual life together
- Easily express affection to each other
- Enjoy restful nights cuddling together
- Play with each other
- Enjoy vacation time together
- Enjoy your meals together
- Manage the importance of work together and take the time needed to make your relationship work
- Manage the maintenance and care of your car efficiently together
- Enjoy physical activities/sports together
- Successfully implement the decisions that you make together
- Touch and caress each other's body and share those sensations with each other

How's your synergy doing?

In the next section, discover our journey on the path of the body.

I'm Right...You Need to Change

Our Journey on the Path of the Body

Our journey on the path of the body has been the easiest journey for Ron and me. We came together with a high level of synergy in many areas. Our biggest challenge showed up in the area of managing money. The table that follows illustrates for each area of the body our initial level of synergy, the level of synergy we experienced when we first got together. It also shows how that level evolved after we did our individual and our couple's work. We again use the Synergy Continuum to indicate our synergy levels. As you will recall, when we either "accept/honor" or "agree" with our partner's position, we create synergy. Of those two, agreement creates the greater synergy. When we "disagree with" or are "in contempt for" each other's position, on the other hand, we create separation in the relationship. Of those two, being in contempt creates the greater separation. You will notice that very few areas on the path of the body created separation in our relationship. We now discuss each one of these areas.

Areas of the Body	Synergy Level at the Beginning of Our Relationship	Synergy Level After We Did Our Healing Work
Day-to-day living	In agreement	In agreement
Participation in the community	In agreement	In agreement
Entertainment	In agreement	In agreement
Financial	In contempt	In agreement
Children	Not applicable	Not applicable
Sexuality	In disagreement	Accept/honor
Expressing affection physically	Accept/honor	Accept/honor

Areas of the body	Synergy Level at the Beginning of Our Relationship	Synergy Level After We Did Our Healing Work
Sleeping habits	In agreement	In agreement
Playing	In disagreement	In agreement
Vacation	In disagreement	Accept/honor
Food	In agreement	In agreement
Work: managing the importance of it	In agreement	In agreement
Car	In agreement	In agreement
Bodies: Taking care of them	Accept/honor	Accept/honor
Implementation of decisions	In agreement	In agreement
Feeling sensations in our body	In disagreement	Accept/honor

Day-to-day living

Day-to-day living has always been easy for us. We have similar expectations in terms of cleanliness; we like our house clean and we easily share tasks. We agreed early on that I would do the cooking and Ron would wash the dishes. This arrangement has worked well for us. We share all the other tasks and do them as needed.

When we first started living together, we noticed that we had both been using the same brand of toothpaste and shampoo. What are the odds of this happening when you consider the number of brands available on the market? This synergy of toothpaste and shampoo symbolizes our day-to-day living. We share similar habits, needs and wants.

Participation in the Community

Because of our work, Ron and I spend 24 hours a day together, 7 days a week. During that time, we spend a lot of time in the company of other people. We both enjoy and require significant amounts of quiet time alone. When our work is done, we like to read or simply relax. For this reason, our participation in the community has been at a minimum.

Entertainment

Ron and I enjoy the same type of entertainment. We like to go to the movies and to jazz clubs. We enjoy visiting museums and get easily overwhelmed if the visit lasts more than a few hours. We can only take so much sensory stimulation at a time. We also enjoy biking together. In short, our interests are very similar.

Financial: How We Manage Money Together

Initially, Ron and I had very different perspectives on money. Ron believed that the universe would always supply him with everything he needed. I, on the other hand, believed that we had to take responsibility for our own financial success by saving money for retirement, for example. This issue was intrinsically linked to the area of developing a vision, goals and a plan mentioned in Chapter 4, The Path of the Mind.

When we initially broached the subject of money, we had powerful arguments. Ron accused me of a lack of faith in God. From his perspective, I was too materialistic and didn't trust in the spiritual law of abundance. I, on the other hand, believed that Ron was irresponsible and immature and that he didn't want to take responsibility for generating abundance in his life. We were angry at each other. When we decided to go within to discover what was going on inside each one of us, we found that wounds had to be healed. Ron's core wound, as mentioned earlier, was a belief that he wasn't good enough and, therefore, didn't deserve abundance in his life. My core wound was related to not experiencing support from my father in the pursuit of my dreams.

Only after releasing the emotional charge from those wounds were we able to identify our true financial needs. By freeing the inner child, the adult could emerge from within each one of us. We now share a strategy on how we manage money and how we want to generate abundance in our life.

Sexuality

Ron and I have very different sexual needs and wants. When we first got together, we disagreed on how often to make love. If I wanted to make love and Ron didn't, I experienced rejection. Hidden within the experience of rejection was a feeling of shame: I wasn't good enough, and that was why Ron didn't want to make love with me. When I could rise to a higher level of consciousness, I knew that that wasn't true. The fact was he had less libido than I did. My judgment was that his lack of interest was a result of my own deficiencies; I must be too fat or not feminine enough. I still remember feeling the pain in my body.

I decided to go within and to find the source of that pain. I recalled the numerous times when I wanted to talk to my father about my day at school or to get him involved in a conversation. I really didn't care what we talked about, I merely wanted his interest and attention. I remember not being able to connect with him and the ensuing judgments that I made about myself. I wasn't lovable, I wasn't pretty enough, I didn't know what to do to make my dad love me. Remembering these events, I re-experienced the pain held in my body since childhood. The pain was excruciating and I felt it in every part of my being.

I shared those experiences with Ron. He held me as I relived in my body the numerous attempts I had made over the years to connect with my dad. Finally able to separate my childhood pain from my adult experience, I came to the realization that I was responsible for getting my sexual needs and wants met. If I wanted to make love, I could ask for it and make it happen. I didn't have to wait for Ron to want it as much as I did.

From that moment on, Ron and I have lived in peace and in acceptance of our different sexual needs and wants. If and when

I want to make love, I ask for it. Because of our commitment together and of his love for me, Ron is usually more than willing to accommodate me.

Expressing Affection Physically

Ron and I are also very different in this area. I love to touch and hug often during the day. Ron enjoys it also, but to a lesser degree. We both ask for what we need and for what we want. I often say, "I need a hug" or "Can you hold me?" Or, I'll simply ask for a kiss. This has worked well for us. We both get what we want and need by taking responsibility for asking. We accept and honor our differences.

Sleeping Habits

Ron and I both have unusual sleeping habits. We often get up in the middle of the night and work on the computer or read. Because of our flexible work schedule, this hasn't been a problem. As we are often able to sleep in in the morning, we do enjoy cuddling and snuggling together. This helps us stay connected to each other and calms and nurtures our bodies and souls.

Playing

I remember the first time Ron came to Montreal with me. After the first day, he told me, "If this is who you are, I don't want to be with you." He had experienced his first French gathering. In his eyes, I was obnoxious, loud and out of control. As for me, well, I was having fun. I remember listening to his judgments and then asking him to give me the facts. I laughed a lot, talked with a strong voice and hugged everyone. He looked inside to see what button got pushed. I had reactivated the part of him that wanted to have fun. But he didn't know how to be playful so he experienced anger at his own inability and had projected that anger on me.

This event opened up a new chapter in our ability to play together. When we first met, we were very different. I enjoyed teasing and playing like a child, whereas Ron was more reserved. Teasing for him was disrespectful. After that trip to Montreal, his joyful inner child started showing up. He started teasing and playing with me. Our ability to laugh together and to make fun of ourselves and of each other was uplifting. We noticed how rested and relaxed we felt after spending an hour or so simply playing together. We had moved from disagreement to agreement and had discovered a new way to get closer to each other.

Vacation

New York is one of my favorite cities; I enjoy it with passion. Europe is my favorite continent to visit; I am enthralled by its variety of cultures and art. Ron's dream holiday is New Zealand; he loves its people and their lifestyle.

Planning vacation time together started out as a minefield of endless discussions and frustration for both of us. Our needs and wants were different. Visiting museums and tasting fine foods and wines are some of my favorite activities, while Ron prefers relaxing, enjoying the sun and the people. I was especially adamant that Ron would see it my way. I tried to sell the wonders of New York, the "spiritual dimension" of being immersed in a vibrant and cosmopolitan city. I tried to convince him but to no avail. In his experience, New York was loud and polluted. Why would anyone want to go there? I was disappointed and sad. I held this dream of discovering foreign lands with my beloved. Ron suggested I visit New York by myself.

Reality finally set in. I let go of my dream. I accepted that Ron would probably never enjoy the kind of vacation I wanted. We are now both willing to share each other's preferred holiday spot. We will eventually get to New York, and I am more than willing to visit New Zealand.

Food

Ron and I have similar nutritional needs. We both had been on a high-protein diet for years before we met. Sharing foods together was easy. There was no need for a special menu.

Managing the Importance of Work

Ron and I each had considerable experience in the corporate world. When we met, he managed a golf resort and I had my own consulting firm. We were both familiar with 60 to 75 hours workweeks, but when we met, we wanted none of that any more.

Our priorities in life have always been clear, work is important; it's an opportunity for us to make a difference and to share our talents, but it's not the most important thing in our life. Our life and our spiritual work are a higher priority. Managing the importance of work in our life has never been an issue.

Car

Ron takes care of our car in Kansas City, and I take care of our car in Montreal. This has never been an issue for us.

Taking Care of Your Body

Exercising is a priority for Ron and me. We have different interests and practices, and although we don't agree on types of sports or forms of exercise, we support each other in pursuing our individual interests. Three to four times a week, I walk at a fast pace carrying small weights in my hands. This gives me great pleasure and keeps me in shape. Ron likes competitive sports. He plays racquetball a few times a week and organizes tournaments for the local community center. He also works out at the gym several times a week. Even though we don't enjoy the same types of activities, we are both committed to taking care of our bodies.

How You Implement Decisions

When Ron and I are aligned on a course of action, it is easy for us to share responsibilities and to get things done.

Feeling Sensations in the Body

Both Ron and I have sensitive bodies. We are constantly aware of the physical sensations in our bodies such as pain and pleasure and share that information with each other. In this we are in agreement. However, I am much more comfortable with listening to the emotions held in my body than Ron is. I can easily differentiate whether unease in my stomach is related to the food I ate or to nervousness. Referring to childhood experiences, I would often ask Ron: "What is your body telling you?" He could not answer. I became impatient. I couldn't understand why he couldn't open his body to revealing repressed emotions. I judged him as not wanting to open up. It is often easier for women to link the sensations in their bodies to their emotions. Men often struggle with this.

I learned to accept that Ron was different from me in that area of his life as in many others. Trusting deeply on an intimate level has always been difficult for me. This is often the case for abused children. Acknowledging my lack of trust, letting it go and honoring Ron's experience in his body has been very healing for me. We have moved much closer in how we share the experiences of our bodies. We both feel completely safe in talking about our physical sensations.

Chapter 7

Your Wills Working Together
The Path of the Will

What Is the Path of the Will?

The path of the will is one of focus, determination and courage. The will is that part of us that takes great ideas and transforms them into great realizations. Without our will, there is no impulse to move and to act. We act with our bodies but we need our wills to infuse us with the determination to initiate a specific action, maintain the course and achieve the desired result.

Each one of us has a different level of mastery of the will. For some of us our wills are weak; we fluctuate with the events in our lives. Others have a strong will, nothing can stop them once they have decided on a course of action. They are the people who follow their training program and their diet with a zeal that amazes the rest of us. Once the course of action is established, they maintain their focus and don't even entertain the possibility of altering it.

What is will? Understanding the path of the will is more difficult than understanding the different areas of the path of the body. We can actually see money and can see the system needed to manage it. But how do you see commitment, what does it look like? You can only see the actions that flow from your commitment. Will is an inner force, an inner muscle. We all have it, yet some of us have difficulty accessing it. Why is that? Why do different people have different levels of will and for different areas of their life?

What precedes will? Our will to act stems from our desire for change. You may want to change some part of your life or some part of yourself. For example, if you want to acquire more wealth and/or more "things," you are looking for change in the physical realm. If you want to change your outlook on life, you are looking for change in the mental realm. And if you want to change how you feel about life by increasing your experience of joy, you are looking for change in the emotional realm. But before your will can kick in and generate action of any kind, there has to be a desire for that change, a want or a need.

So the first step to having a will is the desire, want or need for change. The strength of those desires, wants and needs will infuse your will with a corresponding level of determination. In other words, the stronger your desires, your wants and/or your needs, the stronger your determination to achieve them. We have determined from the work that we have done with others and with ourselves, that will is shaped in childhood. Have you noticed how children can easily speak about their wants, their needs and their desires? Have you noticed how difficult it is for them to let go of those same wants, needs and desires, until we train them? The training you give children can be empowering. Comments such as "You can do it," "Keep going, you're doing great," "Look at all that you have achieved, keep going" build their self-confidence and their self-esteem. On the other hand, comments such as " Can't you ever do anything right?" "Why didn't you listen to me?" "You're not good enough" destroy their self-confidence and their self-esteem.

Now, notice the messages you give yourself on a daily basis. Do you have optimistic self-talk or pessimistic self-talk? Do you pat yourself on the back when you do something that works or achieve a goal, or do you tend to dismiss your efforts and your results? Do you tell yourself that you can do whatever you want, or do you doubt your abilities?

These messages you give yourself come from your childhood. They are the tapes you heard and constantly replay, and they impact the strength of your will. Learn to recognize your self-talk. Acknowledge whether it is optimistic or pessimistic. Journal about it and choose to create a positive self-image with optimistic self-talk.

In our coaching work, we often meet individuals with strong wills for following orders or respecting the rules and regulations of a specific social or work environment. However, when it comes to making a change that benefits them personally such as the behavioral changes required to improve their relationship with their partner, they display a total lack of will. How can that be? They have a strong will to do the tasks related to their job, yet, when

I'm Right...You Need to Change

given a weekly assignment to improve their level of intimacy with their partner, for example, they can't do it. It appears that they are suffering from some form of paralysis of the will.

When we pursue this matter, we often discover that as children, these same individuals were discouraged from pursuing their dreams. They were rigorously "trained" to follow orders. As a result, they have now integrated within their Ego structure a will that kicks into action when called upon to follow orders. However, when a natural want, need or desire shows up from within, the will is on stand-by. Just as they were paralyzed as children in their natural expression of Self wants, needs and desires, the adult remains paralyzed when his/her natural Self wants, needs and desires show up. A great deal of sadness is usually experienced and released when people realize how paralyzed their will is because of childhood wounds. It is sad to have spent most of your life willing for others but unable to will for yourself.

Your partner will likely have a different level of willpower as well as willpower for different things than you. Differences in willpower do not affect the synergy of the couple when the action being willed is individualized. In other words, whether or not you exercise will not affect your synergy with your partner as long as your exercise regime does not include an agreement to do it with your partner. But if you have an agreement to exercise together three times a week and you start reneging on that agreement, the synergy of your relationship will be negatively impacted.

As with all other paths, communication is the first step in resolving issues related to the will. Talk with your partner about the commitment you made, review it and make modifications, if needed.

Synergy between partners on the path of the will is about aligning your wills. The more you share similar commitments and similar levels of determination to achieve shared goals, the greater your level of synergy. The path of the will sustains you in all other paths. For example, if you and your partner choose to work on the path of the heart and your will is strong, you will be successful no matter what obstacles show up on the way. For example, you may have identified that expressing anger is an important issue in your relationship and that your inability to do so creates separation. You have agreed on the consequences created by your issue. However, when it comes to committing to a specific course of action, you differ considerably. One of you feels that you should receive coaching on anger management while the other believes that by simply being conscious of the issue, you will slowly acquire the necessary abilities and skills to improve the situation. You are at odds in terms of what you are ready to commit to. You may also disagree on the time you are willing to invest to remedy the situation. In such a situation, your challenge becomes an opportunity to align your wills around an action plan that will call forth from both of you a similar level of determination.

Synergy of the will is definitely the most powerful form of synergy available to two partners. With willpower, you can achieve anything! If you are lacking a vision or goals, your will gives you the determination to develop one. If you are having emotional issues your will supplies you with the courage to do your healing work. For this reason, it is of the utmost importance that partners focus on increasing their level of willpower together.

There are many opportunities to create synergy with your partner on the path of the will. These opportunities reside in the areas listed below. We will discuss each one in the pages that follow.

- Commitments in life (making commitments to do certain things)
- Following through on commitment (doing what needs to be done to honor the commitment)
- Leadership role in making the relationship work
- Commitment to the relationship
- Following through on commitments to the relationship (doing what needs to be done to honor the commitment to the relationship)

The Areas of Synergy in Your Relationship

Commitments in Life (Making Commitments to Do Certain Things)

Making a commitment is agreeing in the present to do something in the future. When you make a commitment, you give your word. You become morally and emotionally obligated. Making a commitment is a choice. You cannot make a commitment unless you are free to do so. Making a commitment under duress is not a commitment; it is bribe, manipulation or blackmailing. If you are not making a free choice when you commit to doing something, don't make the commitment. If you are making a commitment to please someone else or to achieve a different goal than the one stated, recognize your true motives and either make the commitment as planned or choose not to make it.

Honesty with oneself is essential when making a commitment. Recognize what is motivating you to give your word; be honest with yourself. Know that if your motivation is to please someone else, you may feel resentment later on. Know also that if when making a commitment you are pursuing goals different from those stated, you may not achieve them. For example, your husband wants to go on a golfing trip. He wants to go with some of his buddies. You are not happy about it because you would much rather go on a trip to Europe to visit museums and tour castles. Nevertheless, you accept his trip in the hope that he will later accept to go with you. If that is your real motivation, speak to him about it. Negotiate with him. Bring it in the open. Don't commit to taking care of the kids, to supporting him in taking his golf trip if you are expecting something in return without speaking clearly about your expectations. A commitment has to be upfront and honest, including bringing the motivations out into the open. Share with your partner why you are making the commitment. Is it because you want to do it for yourself or do you have some other motivation?

Some people find it easy to make commitments. Others put off making commitments time and time again. They may be afraid of giving their word because they believe that they will be trapped or because deep down they do not believe they are good enough to follow through. They may also not want to commit because they do not trust that others will follow through. The ability to make a commitment is an expression of maturity. It takes maturity to recognize what your true needs and wants are. It takes maturity to recognize that to satisfy those needs and wants, you need to take action. It takes maturity to recognize that you are responsible for taking action.

If making commitments is difficult for you or your partner, some hidden childhood wound is probably stopping you. The ability to make commitments is a learned behavior. Look in your childhood for the source of your difficulty in this area. It may be in your models (parents or educators), or it may be in a decision you made or a belief you hold about yourself resulting from some form of childhood trauma. Maybe your parents never kept the commitments they made to you and you are still holding on to the sadness and disappointment you experienced then. Or maybe there were no consequences when you didn't keep your commitments as a child. Take the time to work this out. Choose to revisit your childhood experiences, identify the wounds you incurred and review the beliefs you took on about making commitments.

Little will change or improve in your life if you cannot make commitments, including your relationship. Learn to make commitments with your partner, feel the excitement that you share, learn from your broken agreements and remain compassionate and loving as you increase your ability to make commitments together.

Following Through on Your Commitments (Doing What Needs to Be Done to Honor Your Commitment)

Making commitments is the first step in generating change in your world. The hardest and most important part comes afterwards. After giving your word, you either follow up on what you agreed to do or you don't. If you follow up on your commitments, you experience the satisfaction of honoring your word and achieving your goal. If you don't, you may experience sadness, fear, anger or shame. You may also act as if you did not really make the commitment, as if you didn't have a choice but were forced into the commitment. You may forego taking responsibility for your actions

I'm Right...You Need to Change

altogether. "Well, I didn't understand it that way," "I didn't think it meant all the time," "It's not that important anyway."

As mentioned earlier, making commitments is a sign of maturity, and so is keeping them. Acknowledging the truth about how you made a commitment is healing. If you can acknowledge to yourself the truth about what happened, you can dig deeper within yourself and unveil your inner process. Acknowledging the truth is freeing, but only if the truth is stated without shame. Blaming yourself for making commitments that you did not keep reinforces your inner negative beliefs about yourself, your pessimistic self-talk. You did not respect your commitment is a fact but blaming yourself for it and experiencing guilt or shame is based on a judgment that you hold about yourself. The judgment that you have of yourself may be what's behind your difficulty in keeping your commitment.

To modify behaviors that don't work, start by embracing them. Behaviors that don't work stem from negative beliefs you have about yourself and from hidden childhood wounds. The hidden motivations and wounds will only be revealed when you are willing to accept your behaviors with love and compassion.

Refusing to admit that you broke your commitment by finding excuses or blaming yourself for not respecting your commitment are two sides of the same coin. They are both based on judgments rather than facts. In the first case, you are finding fault with the commitment. In the second, you are finding fault with yourself. Healing never comes out of empowering your judgments by believing them. Healing occurs when you openly and honestly acknowledge the facts of a situation. You broke your commitment, that's a fact; that is the truth. Speaking the truth is liberating. Sit with that statement; notice what your thoughts are and what your feelings are. Speaking the truth about your commitments is the first step in creating synergy with your partner in this area.

If both of you find it easy to make commitments and keep them, you are creating constant synergy of intention as well as of action. However, if one or both of you have difficulty making and keeping commitments, sit down and talk about what the real issues are. Remember, you can generate more joy and excitement for yourself when you create synergy with your partner.

Leadership Role in Making Your Relationship Work

Who usually asks for timeout or for special time to work out relationship issues? Is it you? Is it your partner? Who plans or initiates activities to create synergy, activities such as doing a house project together, planning a trip together or buying some new furniture to improve the comfort and appearance of your home.

Someone has to take leadership in making your relationship work. Is it always the same person or do you share this responsibility equitably? Talk about this with your partner. Acknowledge the truth about who takes responsibility for supporting the relationship. This is an important task for your relationship. Express gratitude to the person who is doing it. Without someone taking leadership in making the relationship work, there would be no relationship.

Women have traditionally played that role and men have traditionally resented the fact that their partners want to talk about the relationship. But things are changing. More and more, men are willing to initiate taking care of their relationships. If you are committed to the relationship, share that leadership role with your partner. Remember, the relationship is a third entity that needs attention and careful nurturing to strive. Create synergy with your partner by sharing that role.

Commitment to the Relationship

How committed are you to the relationship? Do you take it for granted or do you constantly remind yourself and your partner of its importance in your life? The vows you made aren't enough to sustain your commitment, and simply reminding yourself of them is not sufficient to create a successful relationship with your partner.

If having a fulfilling intimate relationship is an important part of your life plan, renew your commitment to it frequently through action. Organize special moments with your partner to recommit to the relationship. Plan a special dinner or create your own ritual. It can be a yearly trip or a yearly retreat that you take with other couples.

When you renew your commitment, you are breathing new life into your relationship. You and your partner are reminding each other of what is important in life. As you renew your commitment, be specific about what you are committing to. Identify the behaviors that you choose to share together (example, we are committed to speaking the truth at all times), state the goals that you are supporting together (example, we will have three children) and identify the level of priority that you are giving this relationship (example, our relationship is our first priority).

Is your relationship the most important part of your life? Say it. Does it come before everything else in your life? Does it come before your career or your other personal interests? Say it. Where does your relationship fit in the grand scheme of things?

A discussion with your partner about the level of priority of your relationship compared to the other priorities in your life will clarify any ambiguity related to your levels of expectations. The higher the level of priority of your relationship, the higher the level of intimacy and of synergy between you and your partner. It's your choice. What do you want in your life?

Following Through on Commitments to the Relationship

Many of the comments mentioned under (Following Through on Your Commitments) apply here. Following through on your commitments about your relationship will create greater synergy between you and your partner than following through on any other commitment in your life. It makes sense! The more you follow through on what you agreed to do for the relationship, the more you take care it. You are treating it as a third entity with distinct needs, and you are meeting those needs. The more you invest in your relationship, the greater the rewards in intimacy and in shared joy and love. Be vigilant; never take your relationship for granted. Never take your commitment for granted!

YOUR SYNERGY CHECKLIST
REMEMBER:
You can increase your synergy on the path of the will if you:
- Make commitments in life with your partner (exercise, vacations, etc.)
- Follow through on your commitments with your partner
- Share the leadership role with your partner in making the relationship work

- Commit to making your relationship a priority in your life (the higher the level of priority, the greater the potential for synergy)
- Follow through on your commitment to making your relationship a priority in your life (do what needs to be done)

How's your synergy doing?

In the next section, we discuss our journey on the path of the will.

I'm Right...You Need to Change

Our Journey on the Path of the Will

Like most couples, Ron and I have stronger willpowers in certain areas of our life than in others. When a decision is made in those "stronger" areas, moving forward is usually easy. The table that follows illustrates, for each area of the will, our initial level of synergy, the level of synergy that we experienced when we first got together. It also shows how that initial level evolved after we did our individual and our couple's work. We again use the Synergy Continuum to indicate our synergy levels. As you will recall, when we either "accept/honor" or "agree" with our partner's position, we create synergy. Of these two, agreement creates the greater synergy. When we "disagree with" or are "in contempt for" each other's position, on the other hand, we create separation in the relationship. Of those two, being in contempt creates the greater separation. You will notice that we were in disagreement on many of the areas on the path of the will. We now discuss each one of these areas.

Areas of the Will	Synergy Level at the Beginning of Our Relationship	Synergy Level After We Did Our Healing Work.
Commitments in life	In disagreement	In acceptance
Follow-up on commitments in life	In disagreement	In acceptance
Leadership role in making relationship work	In disagreement	In acceptance
Commitment to the relationship	In acceptance	In acceptance
Follow-up on commitments to the relationship	In disagreement	In agreement

Commitments in Life

It is generally easy for me to make commitments. It isn't as easy for Ron. When we first got together, he kept a back door open on some commitments, never fully committing inside of himself. As a result, we had numerous disagreements on this issue. I had strong judgments about Ron's inability to commit with clarity and determination. I reacted to Ron the same way that I had reacted to my father's lack of commitment to me. I had been disappointed with my father's fluctuating commitments. He would promise one thing and deliver something totally different. When I completed my bachelor's degree, for example, he talked about sending me to Europe for a few weeks with my mother. The following week our trip was rerouted to Barbados for a week. Ultimately, my mother and I ended up in Montreal for a weekend! I had experienced sadness and frustration with my father as a child and I now transferred those emotions to my experience of Ron's level of commitment.

Ron's difficulty with commitment stemmed from his childhood. He had not experienced being fully supported in his choices as a child and had lost the desire and ability to make choices and therefore to make commitments. We both worked on our wounds and have come to a place of acceptance. Our processes for making commitments are different. Yet, we now experience compassion for ourselves and for each other. We both know that as mature adults, we need to make commitments in life. Reinforcing our ability to commit and increasing our level of compassion for our individual processes has brought us much closer.

Following Through on Commitments

As a child, Ron gave up on what he wanted for himself; he stopped making choices. As an adult, when he did make choices and expressed them as commitments, he often experienced resentment at having made those choices. In the first years of our relationship, we often disagreed on the commitments we had made. I thought we were both committed in the same way to doing certain things. Ron, on the other hand, experienced making a commitment for me. He would agree in words but disagree in intention, and his resentment would show up a few weeks later. I remember one instance involving buying furniture for our living room. I liked a leather chair and sofa and Ron agreed to purchase them. My experience was that we had discussed it at length and that Ron had willingly approved the purchase. A few weeks after purchasing the set of sofa and chair, Ron expressed his anger at having been "forced" into buying it. In fact, he had given up his opinion about the purchase to please me.

I remember experiencing disappointment and sadness with what I judged to be Ron's inability to own up to his commitments. I had thoughts that he was immature and weak. Why couldn't I be with a man who knew his mind? Memories of my own childhood came to consciousness, and I re-experienced feelings of frustration and of sadness with my father.

By working through our own wounds, we have evolved as a couple. When we now make commitments together, we are both conscious of the need to be totally honest about what is real to us. Ron has improved his ability to speak the truth about what he is willing to commit to and I have increased my level of compassion and patience for his process. We have become better partners through our willingness to heal our inner wounds.

Leadership Role in Making the Relationship Work

Our core wounds really showed up in this area. Ron's core wound was around not being good enough. As a result, he had learned to follow the flow of life. If he did not strive to achieve goals, subconsciously he thought that he wouldn't experience failure. For this reason, he did not often take leadership in making the relationship work.

One of my core wounds was related to not receiving support for my dreams and my wants. I had been disappointed time and time again as a child. My thoughts and dreams had never been taken seriously or even acknowledged. As a result, I learned to create what I wanted; I developed skills in planning and visioning. Early in the relationship, I often took the leadership role in making things happen.

Ron viewed my ability to plan and my desire to make things happen as a control issue, judging me as being controlling and wanting to tell him what to do. I perceived his lack of leadership and planning abilities as a resistance to taking responsibility. I judged him once again as immature and weak. This was a significant problem in our relationship originally. Since then, we have talked about the underlying core issues. We have revealed the pain that we were still holding on to, the pain that stifled our ability to be compassionate and to take leadership in making our relationship work. We have learned to understand the motivation behind the behaviors, and we have learned to share the role of taking leadership in our relationship.

Commitment to the Relationship

Ron and I came together with an equal level of commitment to the relationship, identifying it as our first priority. We recognized early on that being in a committed relationship was the best way for us to do our spiritual work, and we were committed to doing that work both individually and together.

As mentioned, our family histories are very different. I am the oldest of four children; Ron is an only child. I have raised three children; Ron has had no children. Because of those different experiences, it has always been easier for me to commit to a relationship. Ron is still learning to expand his experience of the single child by opening up to sharing his life with a partner.

Following Through on the Commitment to the Relationship

Ron had issues around following through on any commitment, including his commitment to the relationship. Having given up his power to choose as child, he learned to second-guess his decisions as an adult. So even though he stated a commitment to the relationship, and believed it when he made it, he questioned the commitment after the fact. Ron's healing process took several years. He had to acknowledge his right to have needs and wants and to have dreams. He also had to re-experience the confusion and sadness that he experienced as a child at not being supported in his wants, needs and dreams. He had to become his own parent and to validate his adult needs and wants. Only when he had completed that process was he able to make peace with his commitments and actively believe and embody his word through action.

Through this process, I learned to open my heart. I increased my level of compassion and developed patience. I also had to heal remnants of the pain and anger that I had experienced when my father would change his original commitments. These experiences had generated fear of abandonment. By not following up on his commitments to me, my father had in fact abandoned me. I re-experienced that fear with Ron.

As we build our relationship, our commitment to each other grows. As we are willing to divulge our fears and our wounds, we are increasing our ability to use our wills as partners.

Chapter 8

Your Spirits Working Together
The Path of Spirit

What Is the Path of the Spirit?

The physical dimension of existence can be easily acknowledged. So can the emotional, the mental and the will dimensions. We can see our bodies. We can feel our emotions.

We can hear and read thoughts. We know from experience that the will exists; we can observe it in action.

But the spiritual dimension of existence is a matter of faith. When we attempt to prove the existence of the spiritual dimension, whether in the form of a specific higher being, a specific religion or as spirit moving through us, we find that there are as many definitions as there are movements and religions. Some people dispute the very existence of a higher being, of spirit, or even of a spiritual dimension of our existence.

Ron and I chose to believe in the spiritual dimension of our existence. We experience it in our lives working on a day-to-day basis. As we pray and meditate together each day, we enjoy the effects such practices have on our relationship. We grow closer as a couple as we become more adept in our spiritual practices. It is our experience; it is our choice. These are our beliefs.

The spirit within us enables us to transcend our limited personal consciousness by experiencing a connectedness to a higher consciousness. Most of us are caught up in our day-to-day activities. We live at a frantic pace, taking care of a family, going to work, interacting with people, and as a result we often lose our self. We lose our ability to reflect on our life and to go within. We are entangled in the outside world, in the "doing" instead of in the "being," which is the connectedness to a Higher Self.

The spiritual dimension speaks to the truth of who we are, of our ability to be. Our "beingness" goes beyond doing and having. Doing and having are transient experiences; they don't last. Being, on the other hand, is a permanent experience of who we truly are.

When you can take time for yourself and simply be with yourself, you can begin to experience the core of your being. You can begin to get in touch with that part of yourself that transcends time and space, that part of yourself that is connected to what is immutable, to a "Higher Being" energy.

The outside world is always changing; the love and light within each one of us is everlasting. But you cannot access that part of yourself if you don't direct your attention to it. What you focus on, you get more of! Since it is so easy to be distracted by what is outside of ourself, it takes strong commitment and dedication to focus on the spiritual part of ourselves. The spirit within you enables you to connect to a transcendental form of understanding. Through your spirit, you transcend your limited Ego consciousness and expand your awareness of the truth that is behind any given situation.

Let's take an example. You and your partner are having a recurring discussion; you never seem to find a solution. You are revisiting a constant in your marriage: disagreement over how you manage the family budget. You take some time out and retreat to your room to pray, meditate and ask for guidance. You ask for inspiration to get to the bottom of the issue. All of a sudden you remember a childhood event: Your parents were fighting over the family budget. You remember that they constantly fought over financial priorities. You remember the fear. Suddenly, you understand what you are really fighting about many years later; it is your way to heal that childhood wound. You are still carrying the fear you experienced every time your parents fought over money issues. Instead of looking at the facts in your present situation, that there is more than enough money to go around, you have created an imaginary crisis situation so you can heal that past wound. You are filled with gratitude for the insight. You step out of your room and share your insight with your partner.

Prayer and Meditation

Through prayer and meditation, you are able to access a higher part of yourself, that spiritual part of yourself that brings a transcendental form of understanding. The spirit within us connects us to a higher power. Throughout the ages men have given different names and attributes to that higher power. For you

I'm Right...You Need to Change

that power can be God, or Jesus or Yahweh. The name is your choice. Our consciousness of a higher power comes from our own acknowledgment that we are limited in our personal day-to-day experience. Much goes on beyond our control and our grasp. Many events are inexplicable; many phenomena are beyond our logical understanding and explanation. Our consciousness of a higher power is also an acknowledgement that a higher intelligence is at work in our life; an underlying organization of principles that guides our experience on this planet.

You may be facing a crisis in your life and may have depleted all your apparent resources in trying to resolve it. Through prayer and meditation, you surrender that issue to a higher power, trusting that all will be well. You choose hope and trust, understanding that you create as you believe. You choose to believe that all is possible and that you will receive your highest good. Have you ever experienced wanting something desperately? Have you ever experienced not getting it and being deeply disappointed? And have you then experienced that in hindsight what you did get in a specific situation was better for you than what you had originally wanted? We certainly have.

If you believe that there is no hope and that trust is a naïve way of viewing life, your life will prove you right. Remember, what you believe, you create. Choose to believe what supports you. The path of the spirit is about the relationship you establish with that higher source of being. What beliefs do you hold dear to your heart? Is your God part of all that exists, even a part of you? Is he a God that judges your day-to-day actions with severity? God for you may be a being of compassion and of love. What do you believe about God and how does that serve you?

Manifesting Your Relationship with a Higher Being

The path of the spirit also includes how we chose to manifest our relationship with a higher power. What practices do you embrace? Are you an active participant in this relationship with your God? Do you go to church, pray and/or meditate? Do you have other rituals that you perform to deepen and develop that relationship with your God.

Do you share those beliefs and practices with your partner? Creating synergy with your partner on this path is about your spirits working together. You and your partner may have different practices and beliefs. That isn't a problem as long as you respect and honor each other's beliefs and practices. Through honoring each other, you are creating synergy in your relationship. However, the synergy that you create together can expand if you share beliefs and if you have common spiritual practices.

How we relate to God is also reflected in how we relate to others and to ourselves. Are we victims or responsible participants in life? Some of the teachings and dogmas upheld by certain churches or spiritual organizations disempower their members. You are told that your will needs to be subservient to God's will as represented by the leaders of the church. Members of such communities are stripped of their right to discern what are judgments as opposed to facts, stripped of their right to make choices other than those upheld as the "right" choices by the religious leaders. Such individuals lose all sense of personal responsibility. If they have no choice, they cannot be responsible for what they do. They are, in fact, victims of their belief system. In such situations, your relationship with God has affected your relationship with yourself. You are no longer responsible for the choices you make in your life.

Impact of Dogmas

Be careful when you choose a religion or a spiritual organization. Think of the impact the teachings and dogmas have on your experience as a human being. Are you becoming a copy of the leaders of the organization or are you respected and honored for your God-given individuality? Remember, all religious books were written by men. Therefore, these books offer a very "human" and therefore limited perception of the truth of God. Make sure that you are supported in manifesting your creative essence instead of being expected to follow someone else's dreams and beliefs.

In fact, your spiritual beliefs and practices can either expand or diminish your experience of yourself. If your relationship with yourself is affected negatively by your spiritual beliefs and practices, that is, if you hold yourself as disempowered and subservient to some higher power, your relationship with others will be affected in the

I'm Right...You Need to Change

same way. If you are not responsible for your actions because they are dictated from outside of yourself, how can you be responsible for your actions towards others? You may be able to justify your anger, your rigidity, your closed heartedness by saying, "That's what the Book says," "That's what the minister or priest said," but in doing so you have lost your ability to discern what is warranted in each situation and you are losing your ability to discover the true spiritual meaning, the gold hidden within each crisis.

Let's look at an example. You are a member of a religious organization that holds that women should stay at home and raise children. That is their God-given duty. You have a daughter who has a passion for science and wants to study astrophysics. You try to force her to conform to your concept of what a woman should be. In doing so, you have lost touch with your daughter; you do not see her for who she is.

God speaks to each one of us in different ways. Simply notice the number of beliefs systems, religious or spiritual organizations in existence on this planet. The higher being speaks to us through the heart of others and through the passions of others. If you have a spiritual belief system that reflects God's love and compassion, the teachings and dogmas associated with that belief system will enable you to demonstrate love and compassion for all human beings, including those who hold belief systems that are different from yours.

If you blindly follow teachings and dogma without noticing how those are affecting the type of human being you are becoming, you are giving up your ability to discern. You can no longer perceive options or truths outside of your belief system and you are missing specific opportunities in each situation. Convinced of the righteousness of your beliefs and of your judgments, you have lost your ability to question yourself. Indeed, you are no longer on a spiritual path. You have become a religious robot programmed to follow orders. You have lost your own individual essence and in the process you may have lost your humanity.

The spiritual path is inclusive. If God is everything, you want to increase your ability to embrace the human experience in all its manifestations. If God is loving, you want to increase your ability to have compassion for all human beings. The qualities you see in your God are a reflection of the qualities you will espouse in yourself. If your God is compassionate, it will be easier for you to be so with others. If your God is forgiving, you will be reminded of your own ability to forgive and if your God is righteous, you will tempted to be righteous yourself. Remember; be careful what spiritual or religious system you embrace. Choose one that increases the level of love and of joy in your life.

There are many opportunities to create synergy with your partner on the path of spirit. These opportunities reside in the areas listed below. We will discuss each one in the following pages.

- Spiritual belief system and beliefs (understanding of God, metaphysics and religious dogmas)
- Spiritual practices: prayer, meditation, etc.
- Communication about spiritual beliefs
- Taking responsibility for your actions
- Taking responsibility for your experience (your shadow parts)
- Caring and compassionate attitude towards others and towards yourself
- Forgiveness towards others and towards yourself
- Giving others acknowledgment
- Acknowledging mistakes and shortcomings
- Honesty
- Loyalty
- Respect

The Areas of Synergy in Your Relationship

Spiritual Beliefs (Understanding of God, Metaphysics and Religious Dogmas)

What is your understanding of God? Are you a member of a religious organization with a specific system of beliefs and very defined dogmas? Are you more inclined to follow your own set of spiritual beliefs? Or do you not have any specific beliefs about God? If you don't have a relationship with God or a higher power, how do you source yourself? Where do you go for insight about life and for courage when life unravels in unpredictable and painful ways? Having a spiritual belief system, whatever that may be for you, is about establishing a conscious relationship with a source. That source may be inside of you, if you believe that God is part of you, or it may be outside of you, if you believe that God is an entity separate from your own.

How is your spiritual belief system serving you?
- Do your beliefs increase your ability to love and to have compassion for others?
- Do your beliefs increase your sense of empowerment?
- Do your beliefs expand your consciousness? Are you open to all the possibilities in your life?
- Do your beliefs support you in being the best that you can be?

You may not think that you are free to choose your own belief system. Your parents or the educational institutions you attended may have provided you with a specific belief system. The truth is that you do have a choice! You have the same choice in the spiritual realm as you have in the emotional realm, for example. Just as you now know that you can re-educate yourself and learn to open up, to reveal emotions that are hidden in your heart, the same is true for your choice of spiritual beliefs. You have a choice in what you choose to believe. As a child you didn't; but as an adult you do.

As mentioned earlier, question your spiritual beliefs. Do they serve you well? Do they make you more understanding and compassionate or more judgmental? Your belief system will either increase or jeopardize your level of synergy with your partner. If your belief system is one of compassion and understanding, you will tend to express those attributes with your partner. If your belief system is one of judgment, rigidity and righteousness, you will tend to reflect that with your partner as well as with other family members and friends.

Find an empowering belief system and share it with your partner. He or she may embrace similar spiritual beliefs. Having a common set of beliefs is one of the most powerful means of increasing synergy. You can increase your level of synergy even if you don't share the same beliefs by accepting and embracing your partner's choice of beliefs. Every time you embrace your partner's thoughts and actions, you are expressing love and acceptance. The expression of love and acceptance is the single most powerful way to increase synergy. However, if you can share spiritual beliefs with your partner, this can lead you to share spiritual practices together.

Spiritual Practices (Prayer, Meditation)

There are countless forms of spiritual practices. They reflect the spiritual beliefs from which they stem. Some of them are empowering; they remind us of our own divinity, of our own higher power and consciousness. Other practices are disempowering; they enslave us to a God outside of our Self and reinforce the belief that we are limited in power and sinful in nature. Such spiritual practices do not lead to increased synergy with your partner because they limit the ability of each partner to create the life that he or she wants.

The spiritual practices that we are referring to in this chapter are those that allow each individual to uncover more of his or her true Self. How do your spiritual practices affect your experience of yourself? Are you reminded of your inherent goodness and supported in achieving your dreams? Or are you reminded that you are powerless and sinful? Choose spiritual practices that support you in becoming more powerful. Once you have done so, look at how you share those with your partner. Do you pray with your partner, do you meditate together?

When you pray together, you remind yourselves that there is a higher form of consciousness that transcends your day-to-day preoccupations. You focus on that higher consciousness. When you pray together, you affirm your commitment to living every day

I'm Right...You Need to Change

on that higher plane of consciousness. When you pray together, you affirm the truth about life. You affirm your belief that the natural state of being human is a state of love and of compassion. When you pray together, you deny the illusion of the Ego, you deny that life is rooted in fear. Praying together brings a state of peace that you share with your partner; you live your day-to-day from that state of consciousness.

Meditation prepares you for prayer. Meditation calms the mind of idle chatter and thereby allows you to focus on that inner part of yourself that knows the metaphysical truth of life and that experiences the connectedness with a higher power. In other words, meditation creates the space to reach out to your own source. Praying establishes that connection to your source.

Share your prayers and meditations with your partner. Invite him or her to practice with you. If that isn't possible, choosing to embrace your partner's spiritual practices, love and acceptance also increases synergy. If you can share spiritual practices with your partner; do so. When you start your day with prayer and meditation, you create a higher consciousness in yourself and in your relationship. You align your focus on a higher consciousness. You remind yourself that your Ego is not in charge and that your focus in life is to create more synergy, love and compassion with your partner. You create a synergy of spirit. The rest of the day flows much more smoothly. Issues are dealt with more expediently and with more love and compassion. In fact, conflicts can be averted altogether.

Communication About Spiritual Beliefs

We are all following our own individualized spiritual path. Even if you and your partner practice the same religion or share similar spiritual beliefs, you have developed your own understanding and experience of that religion or those spiritual beliefs. Take the time to listen to each other. Share your insights; share the struggles of your path. The ability to express clearly to your partner and to listen with compassion to your partner's experience on the spiritual path will bring you closer. You will understand what guides each other's life and you will be a witness to each other's deepening understanding and relationship with God.

As you share your trials and tribulations, your heart will be touched and inspired, you will experience greater depths of intimacy with your partner. Take the time to source yourself with your partner, share your experience of your relationship with a higher being.

Taking Responsibility for Your Actions

Is it easy for you to take responsibility for your actions, or are you constantly coming up with excuses? We are all responsible for our actions. To be able to acknowledge your actions for what they are, and to do so without guilt, shame or fear, requires doing your healing work. If you have trouble acknowledging that you are responsible for your actions, especially actions that have a negative impact on others such as being late, not respecting your commitments or losing control, notice what reasons you come up with. For example, you may say or think, "I was late because there was too much traffic or because I received an important telephone call just before leaving; I just had to take it." Do you believe those reasons? Now, imagine that you have no reasons or excuses and that you simply acknowledge the fact of what you did, simply acknowledging to yourself: I was late. What I did had an impact on others and that impact didn't work for them. Notice what you feel when you simply take responsibility for your actions without judging yourself. Do you experience fear? Do you experience shame? The feeling you experience when you simply acknowledge the fact of what you did is the feeling you are trying to avoid when you make up excuses. That feeling is usually based on a judgment you have about yourself. If you are late, do you have judgments about yourself such as, "I'm inconsiderate or I'm irresponsible," or "No one can depend on me"?

If you are defensive when doing something that doesn't work, stop yourself before you start making excuses or supplying your partner with reasons for your action. Take some time alone and notice the judgments you have about yourself and experience the emotions that accompany those judgments. Journal about incidents in your childhood. Remember when you made similar judgments about yourself. Remember the emotions you felt. For example, as a child, your parents may have impressed upon you the necessity to be on time at all times. They may have reinforced your training by stating that individuals who are late lack respect for others and are irresponsible. You may have developed a fear of being late because you didn't want your parents to judge you as disrespectful and irresponsible. Now as an adult, those response mechanisms kick in every time you are late because they have not been dealt with. In other words, you experienced shame every time your parents reminded you that you were disrespectful or irresponsible so now, as an adult, instead of simply acknowledging the fact that you are late, you try to avoid the experience of shame by finding reasons or excuses for your behavior.

Share those experiences with your partner. By sharing your inner process, you are not only increasing your level of intimacy with your partner, you are also dismantling an emotional and behavioral response mechanism created in your childhood. Every time you bring to light behaviors that stem from your childhood and embrace them with compassion, you are healing them. When you start acknowledging to your partner that you are responsible for your actions, you may initially experience fear, a childhood fear of being blamed or being shamed. But stay with the experience. As you show up willing to share, it will eventually disappear.

When you take responsibility, you become accountable. You cannot deflect or avoid the effect of your actions. If you and your partner learn to take responsibility for your actions as individuals and as a couple, your communications will greatly improve. Issues will be easily resolved; responsibility will no longer be projected on the other. You will also experience an increase in your emotional intimacy. You will no longer come from fear when you discuss a specific situation. Taking responsibility for your actions is freeing. With it comes a feeling of joy, an experience of inner lightness of being. The truth is freeing for one's self. The truth spoken between partners increases intimacy.

Taking Responsibility for Your Experience

Before you attempt to take responsibility for your experience, practice taking responsibility for your actions. Taking responsibility for your actions is much easier to do than taking responsibility for your experience. It is a precursor to it. What's the difference between the two? You take responsibility for your actions when you state clearly that you did or did not do something. For example, as mentioned earlier, you state that you were late by 20 minutes. Or you take responsibility for not cleaning the house or simply acknowledge that you did your part of the chores. Taking responsibility for your actions is focused on what you do out there. Taking responsibility for your experience relates to your inner experience. In other words, you take responsibility for your anger, or for your thoughts in that you hold yourself accountable for what you are experiencing in any given situation. No one is making you have those specific thoughts or emotions.

Have you noticed how people have different opinions about the same event or the same person? You may perceive a certain individual as arrogant while your friend sees him as assertive. Why is that? You and your friend have different opinions and judgments about events and about people because those events and those people resonate within each of you in different ways. For example, you were very outspoken as a child and had opinions about everything. You loved to express yourself. Your mother did her best to teach you to be polite and to be careful about what you said. She may have said, "Be gentle when you speak, young girls are supposed to be gentle. People will think you're arrogant if you keep speaking up this way." You slowly learned to shut down; you learned to curb your opinions and started holding back. In the process of satisfying your mother, you paid a huge price. You deprived yourself of the joy of expressing your thoughts and your ideas, and you felt a lot of anger because of it.

Now fast-forward 20 years. You have a new manager. He's about your age and expresses himself with a great deal of assurance. He pushes your button, your button of repressed ideas and thoughts. You judge him as arrogant, and you experience anger towards him, whereas your friend simply sees that he is assertive. His own upbringing probably supports his opinion.

In that very moment, you have a choice. You can choose to see your boss as the source of your anger, and for that reason make him wrong, or you can choose to take responsibility for what you are experiencing and go within yourself. If you are able to acknowledge that you are creating your own experience of the situation, you will start accessing what is behind your reaction. When you get home that night, journal on the event and ask yourself certain questions. What is it in that man that pushes my buttons? What does he do? Do I do this myself? How do I do it? Do I allow myself to act the way he does? If I don't allow myself to act in the same way, why don't I? The behavior displayed by your new manager to which you react so strongly represents an unhealed part of yourself. As you go about answering those questions, you will find the wound that is at the heart of your reaction and you'll then be able to heal it.

We believe that our mission as human beings is to enlighten ourselves. Enlightening ourselves means bringing light into shadow parts of our self. That is our spiritual journey as human beings; this is our transformational work. Shadow parts are parts of ourselves that are hidden. They may be hidden because you never explored them. Maybe you never had to bring them forth or use them. Or, your parents may have repressed them when you were a child. Whatever the reason, your key to being able to bring those hidden parts of yourself to the light can be found in your reaction when you perceive those same parts in others. For example, if you lack courage on a day-to-day basis and shy away from taking up new challenges, you may judge other people's expression of courage as foolishness and feel anger. If you don't allow yourself to express your anger responsibly, you may have trouble hearing the anger of others and experience fear when it shows up in them or in yourself. If you have low self-esteem, you may experience other people's expression of self-confidence as arrogance. Pay attention to what you react to. Take responsibility for what you experience.

We mentioned on the Path of the Heart in Chapter 5 how others push our buttons and what that means. Let's develop this concept further as an important part of taking responsibility for your experience. Your partner is usually the one who pushes your buttons the most. Because you are vulnerable and because of the love you feel for your partner, your shadow parts are more willing to show up. You feel safer to show all of yourself. However, if you hold your partner responsible for your experience, you forfeit a wonderful opportunity to enlighten yourself. In fact, by attributing the responsibility of your experience to your partner, you are giving away your power to do your work. No one can do our healing work for us. Therefore, taking responsibility for your experience is an essential condition to doing your inner healing work.

Also, by not taking responsibility for your experience, you cause separation instead of synergy with your partner. How does not taking responsibility for one's experience create separation? Let's illustrate this with an example. After being in a committed relationship with your partner for a few years, you start noticing that when your partner asks questions, you get impatient. You have judgments about your partner such as, "Why does he ask questions? Didn't he hear what I just said? He doesn't listen to me." With every judgment, your anger grows. Once again, it is your moment to make a choice. You can start making your partner wrong for asking questions and believe your current judgment about him, or you can go within and have the following conversation with yourself. "My partner has every right to ask questions. Why does that push my button? What is my anger about? Do I give myself the right to ask questions?" By answering these questions, you find out the truth about yourself. You discover that as a child, you asked a lot of questions because you had an inquisitive mind. Your father kept telling you not to ask so many questions; he kept reminding you that you were bothering him. As new questions popped up in your mind, you started repressing them because you didn't want to bother your dad. However, at the same time, part of you was angry at not being able to voice your questions. As an adult, that anger is still inside of you. So, now when your partner asks questions, you judge him in the same way you were judged and you experience the anger you felt for your father when he wouldn't allow your questions. In other words, you are projecting your anger on your partner in order to release it from yourself and heal it.

If you get angry at your partner and make him responsible for your reaction, you create separation by projecting your anger and by holding him in a negative light. When you choose to take responsibility for your reaction and go within to find out what causes your reaction, you build more synergy with your partner. This is especially true if you share your process and your wound with your partner. For, as we have stressed throughout, intimacy is INTO-ME-SEE. You can let your partner see into you when you own your experience of the world and when you are willing to share it. By sharing your own transformational work, you unveil a hidden wound and you enlighten that part of yourself with your partner. What a wonderful way to increase the level of synergy of your relationship on the path of the spirit.

Caring and Compassionate Attitude Towards Others and Yourself

We believe that God is love and compassion and that as humans this is our natural state of being. That does not mean that we should never experience other emotions such as anger, fear and shame. If you have compassion for yourself, you can accept all of who you are, including feeling fear, anger and shame. You can embrace those experiences. As you embrace those experiences and totally surrender to feeling the painful emotions, you start loving yourself. And as you love yourself, you can let the energy contained in those emotions flow through you and be transformed into love.

By contrast, when you resist your inner emotional experience, you become hard and closed. We have observed during coaching sessions that individuals who have little compassion for others often have little compassion for themselves. This is especially true for those who have been raised in a strict and righteous religious system. Having learned that aspects of themselves were evil, they started closing their heart to parts of themselves. We have within us all that exists potentially in all human beings, anger, greed, lust, joy and jealousy, for example. We may choose to curtail some of those attributes and to exhibit others. Nonetheless, they are within each one of us. To believe that some individuals or groups of individuals hold a monopoly on "evil" thoughts and deeds and to judge them as lesser because of that is the greatest experience of arrogance available to mankind. No single individual is totally "evil" or totally "good." It is a sign of spiritual maturity to be able to recognize that all human beings represent both "good" and "evil." Spiritual maturity is achieved when one discovers within all aspects of being human.

Knowing that you have all of those human attributes within you, you have a choice. You can try to control them by establishing an inner policing mechanism to repress those attributes or even negate that they ever existed within you, or you can acknowledge that all those traits are within you and embrace them with your love. For example, when you acknowledge that you have felt jealousy in the past and accept that you may feel it in the future; you are able to feel compassion for someone who feels the same. By contrast, when you judge jealousy as "evil" or "wrong," you become hardened and close your heart, not only to others who feel those feelings but to yourself.

Only when you can acknowledge that as humans we are all the same and embrace all of those attributes within your own self can you experience real compassion for yourself and for others. If you hold your partner with love and compassion, you will accept all of who he or she is.

This does not mean that you tolerate all behaviors. In fact, there is a huge difference between allowing your partner to express feelings of jealousy in a responsible way and allowing your partner to act out feelings of jealousy. In the first case your partner comes to you and says something like, "I notice that I feel jealous when you speak with that person. I needed to share this because it stops me from being open to you." This is responsible communication.

The second way is your partner speaking to you as follows, "Why do you always talk to this person? Are you attracted to him?" Those are not responsible behaviors. Embracing your partner's feelings of jealousy refers to accepting your partner's inner experience of jealousy, not your partner's projection of jealousy on you. Embracing the feelings and the pain experienced by your partner does not mean embracing the acting out of those feelings.

Forgiveness of Others and Yourself

The act of forgiving others and forgiving yourself is intimately linked to the ability to care and have compassion for others and yourself. These are characteristics of an open and loving heart. Forgiveness is a four-part process.

Four-Part Process of Forgiveness Part 1 of forgiveness involves allowing yourself to experience all of your feelings and to hear all of your judgments. Let's use an example to illustrate this. Your partner has been talking about problems in your relationship behind your back. You hear about it through a friend and feel angry and sad. Before doing anything else, take the time to feel those

I'm Right...You Need to Change

feelings, let them flow through your body. You may have thoughts that you have been betrayed, that your partner is not trustworthy. You may have thoughts that your partner feels safer communicating with others than with you.

Journal on the emotions you are experiencing. In this example, allow yourself to feel your anger and sadness and write those emotions down. Identify what is true for you. What doesn't work in your partner's behavior? Is it that your partner talked to someone else about your relationship issues or is that your partner talked to someone else about your relationship issues without telling you about them? What is the truth here? What really hurts?

Part 2 of forgiveness involves reflecting on the situation at hand and looking at your own responsibility in bringing it about. Ask yourself what it says about your relationship that your partner talked to someone else about your relationship issues. Is there something that isn't working? What is it? Do you talk about your issues openly together? If not, why? What does it say about you? For example, you may have a hard time listening to your partner express feelings of sadness or of fear. Your personality may be an impediment to having open and honest communications with your partner on your relationship issues. Consequently, your partner may have felt more comfortable talking to someone other than you. This is not about finding excuses for your partner's behavior. This doesn't take away from the fact that your partner talking to someone else about your relationship issues without sharing them with you first does not work for you. You experience it as creating separation. However, you want to understand and take responsibility for your own behavior that may have enabled these behaviors in your partner.

Get a total perspective on the situation. Events never happen in a vacuum. There are circumstances and forces in place that motivate the choices people make. Some of those forces may be within your partner, others may be within you.

Part 3 is about deciding on a course of action and following through. It is about communicating with your partner about the situation that troubles you. Communicating with the person you believe hurt you is not always essential. Sometimes you can resolve the situation within yourself and choose not to have that person be part of your life any more. Sometimes you may forgive the other and also choose to break the relationship. In the example above, involve your partner and focus on reestablishing the synergistic energy of the relationship. You can sit down with your partner and share your experience. When you do so, state your intention for the discussion. State clearly that you have something to share, that this is difficult for you, that you feel separate from your partner and that you want to recreate intimacy and closeness. When you share your emotions, make sure that you do it in a responsible way. Also take responsibility for what you may have done to bring about the situation. Listen to your partner's point of view and to your partner's emotions. Work on remaining open. Be vulnerable and honest.

Part 4 is about the act forgiving. Forgiveness is a powerful choice. When you forgive, you bring light into pain, you let go of your judgments; you surrender to your feelings. After you have shared your experience with your partner and nothing is left unsaid, forgive your partner and forgive yourself. True forgiveness leads to love. If you don't experience love for your partner after the experience of forgiveness, you have not completely forgiven. Look inside and see if there is any resentment left. You may be holding on to resentment for your partner or for yourself. Share those feelings with your partner. Keep looking within until all that's left is love and compassion.

Your ability to forgive others is a reflection of your ability to forgive yourself. As in the case of having a caring and compassionate attitude, the more you experience those attributes for yourself, the more you can express them for others. If you have difficulty forgiving yourself, look at your childhood for the cause. By becoming conscious of your own humanity, by acknowledging that you are trying your best, and that we are all in the process of learning spiritual lessons, you will know in your heart that you deserve forgiveness. In truth, we are all trying to do what is best according to our conscience. Our consciousness is not always enlightened enough to understand and foresee the consequences of the actions that we take.

Forgiveness paves the way to learning. You can learn when you accept without judgment that you did not achieve the goal you had

I'm Right...You Need to Change

set out to reach. You can learn when you accept without judgment that your actions had a negative effect on someone else. You can learn when you are willing to look within and acknowledge the part of yourself that was driving your behavior.

Within relationships, there are many opportunities to forgive yourself and forgive your partner. Each time you practice forgiveness, you increase the synergy between the two of you. When you forgive yourself, you accept a part of you that you may not have experienced before. When you forgive your partner, you accept and embrace a part of him or her that you may not have experienced before. Forgiveness leads to the discovery of more of yourself and more of your partner, and with discovery and acceptance comes greater love and compassion.

Acknowledging Others

As a management consultant, I often asked senior management teams the following questions:
- Of the total number of hours worked by your employees, what percentage do you believe is productive and efficient?
- What percentage of your communications is used to acknowledge those positive results?

The answers I got were always interesting. Most of the time, managers stated that their employees were productive and efficient at least 80 percent of the time. And yet, when asked what percentage of their communication was directed at those positive results, the answers were usually reversed. That is, 80 percent of the time was spent on talking about what didn't work instead of about what did work.

You cannot build a successful team if you don't hold it that way in your consciousness and your actions. How you hold someone in consciousness is reflected by how you speak to them.

This also holds true for relationships. If you want to create a successful relationship, start acknowledging your partner about what works. The more acknowledgment you give, the more you are feeding the positive image you hold in your mind of your relationship and of your partner. If you are constantly reminding your partner of the things that don't work, you focus your mind and look for things that don't work. Gradually, you start believing that your partner does a lot of things that don't work. Your mind believes what you tell it! So be careful of how you talk to your partner and focus on the positive. If your partner has a behavior that is counterproductive, look for signs of improvement and acknowledge every single step taken by your partner to modify that behavior. The acknowledgment you give will support your partner in maintaining his or her own positive behavior.

The outside reflects the inside. Most people have trouble acknowledging others because they have trouble acknowledging themselves. What are your patterns in terms of self-acknowledgment? Do you have trouble patting yourself on the back? Do you have judgments such as, acknowledging myself is a sign of pride and pride is not good? Learn to acknowledge yourself and to heal what is in the way of doing so. During our coaching sessions, we often discover that what is lurking behind a difficulty to acknowledge oneself is shame. If you believe that you are not good enough or a failure, you will have difficulty in acknowledging that what you did worked. Healing the shame within will enable you to receive acknowledgment from others and from yourself.

You build yourself into what you believe you are. So believe that you are good by acknowledging all those things that you do that work, you will start doing more and more of them. And you will be able to give acknowledgment to your partner.

As with any team, you cannot build success by constantly focusing on mistakes and shortcomings. Instead, you build a good team by focusing on its strengths. Do the same for your relationship, you will discover that you want to spend more time together and that you are becoming better individuals as well.

Acknowledging Your Mistakes and Shortcomings

The easier it is for both partners to acknowledge the successful areas of their relationship and the constructive nature of their behaviors, the easier it is to acknowledge their mistakes and their shortcomings.

Success in life can be measured by whether you are producing the intended result through a chosen behavior. Achieving success is cause for celebration and reinforcement. When you acknowledge your successes on any scale, you are reinforcing the behaviors that produced those successes. Failure to achieve the success anticipated because of mistakes you made or because of your personal shortcomings calls for understanding and learning. Before you can understand the nature of your mistakes or your shortcomings, you must accept that you made a mistake and/or that you did not achieve the anticipated result.

This is often difficult to do. In our sessions, we watch with interest as partners disagree on whose "fault" something was. It's like watching a game of ping-pong. Each partner throws back the ball as quickly as he or she receives it. And the emotional charge keeps growing. Why is it so hard to acknowledge our mistakes and shortcomings? The answer lies in the following questions: What do you think of yourself when you acknowledge that you made a mistake or that you did not achieve the anticipated goal? But more important, what do you feel about yourself?

The answer is shame. We often find that the greater the resistance to acknowledging a mistake, the greater the level of shame. Shame is a combination of a judgment that I am a bad person and the fear that someone will find out how bad I really am. Shame is a devastating experience. It often comes in childhood from having been laughed at or ridiculed for having certain thoughts or feelings or for having done certain things. It may even come from having been looked at in an angry way. Shame is such a powerful experience that we build a maze of defensive beliefs and emotions to protect us from ever experiencing it again.

Even in adulthood, the thought of acknowledging a mistake can bring to the fore the experience of shame. For this reason, it is often impossible to acknowledge our mistakes and shortcomings. Let's have a closer look at this area.

Imagine having a continuous experience of your magnificence as a human being. You experience love for yourself on a continuous basis, reinforcing your positive attributes. You are grounded in your own inner sense of beauty. One day, you do something that doesn't work. You response is, so what? I did something that doesn't work. What can I learn? How can I improve? In other words, you want to increase your positive experience of yourself and are prepared to use your mistake to build on that experience. You want to gain knowledge from your personal shortcoming and develop a new ability, a new skill and a new attitude in life.

Now imagine the flipside. You have such negative beliefs about yourself that you are convinced others will run away if they find out who you really are. You are unconscious of that deep belief and that hidden terror. Imagine how you feel if you make a mistake or don't reach a goal. Out of fear and shame, you find excuses and reasons to explain the mistake, because acknowledging a mistake or a shortcoming is tantamount to admitting that you are as bad as believed. With such a defensive position in place, acknowledging mistakes and shortcomings is impossible.

Partners' ability to acknowledge their mistakes and shortcomings makes traveling on the path of spirit easier. The lessons are more easily learned and mistakes don't need to be repeated. No energy is lost in trying to deflect responsibility and finding an alternative culprit. But more significant, both partners can use their energy to learn whatever lesson is contained in the mistakes made and in their shortcomings. This ability can transform the path of spirit from a primitive tortuous road to a highway of enlightenment.

Honesty

In the Webster dictionary, honesty is defined as "the act of refusing to lie, steal or deceive in any way." It is also defined as "adherence to the facts." In a relationship where the goal is to create higher levels of synergy, honesty about what is true for each of the partners is essential. However, being honest does not mean that you have to share every single thought, judgment, belief, emotion or action. What is important to share are those thoughts, judgments, beliefs, emotions and actions that can either increase your synergy or create separation from your partner.

Let's look at the following example to better understand this. You have noticed that when you and your partner go out for an evening with friends, you have a lot of judgments about how she behaves; you judge her as too loud. When you get home, you start looking at yourself and come to the realization that your partner allows herself to speak with enthusiasm and conviction, something that you have trouble doing due to your upbringing. You share this insight with her. These judgments show up again, each time

I'm Right...You Need to Change

you go deeper into your beliefs about yourself, into your wounds around expressing excitement in life. You don't need to share these judgments every time they show up. You already own them as your own and are doing your transformational work.

Being honest is not easy for everyone. What usually stands in the way of honesty is fear: fear of hurting someone, fear of what the other person will say, fear of how you're going to say what you want to say. It takes courage to be honest. It takes courage to be in an intimate relationship. Think of the consequences of hiding something important from your partner. Think of the loss in emotional intimacy that you are bringing to the relationship. Giving in to fear creates separation with your partner and with yourself.

If you have something to share that you find difficult to say, write down specifically what it is that you want to communicate. Make sure that what you want to say comes from a place of love and compassion. Write down what your fears are and think of ways to manage the possible shutdown of your communication. If you are still uncertain about how to communicate what's true for you, talk to someone who can provide you with advice. This can be a trusted friend, a spiritual guide, a minister or priest, a counselor, a therapist or a transformational coach.

Find a way to communicate with your partner. During coaching sessions we have witnessed partners sharing truths about themselves that they were convinced would provoke a strong and negative reaction from their partner. The truth was that their fear was usually greater than the reaction they got. If you are afraid to talk to your partner, if you have shame or guilt about what you want to talk about, share that with your partner before you start talking. We have found that talking about how you feel before you actually talk goes a long way in relieving the stress you are carrying. After all, the feeling is real, and sharing it is part of being honest.

Nothing compares to honesty when it comes to creating a safe space for your relationship. Such a relationship thrives. As we have mentioned several times in this chapter, the outer reflects the inner. Before you can be honest with your partner, you must be honest with yourself because if you cannot admit to yourself what the truth is, if you have trouble acknowledging your mistakes and shortcomings, you'll have trouble being honest with your partner. Practice honesty with yourself. Be ruthless with your mind. Train it to discern facts from judgments and to simply admit the truth. As you become more honest with yourself you will find it easier to be honest with your partner.

Shame is often the barrier to honesty. That is, you are afraid of your judgments about yourself so you avoid acknowledging all the facts. This is a spiritual training. The spiritual path is about acknowledging the truth at all cost. There can be no light inside of you if there is no truth about who you are. Practice being honest with yourself and your partner. It gets easier as time goes by.

Loyalty

Loyalty is defined in the Webster dictionary as "being faithful to a private person to whom loyalty is due." In a committed relationship, loyalty means acting in accordance with the level of commitment and trust that you agreed to with your partner. In other words, you are loyal to your partner when you respect the vows you made. You are loyal to your partner when you stand by him or her through the good times and the bad times. It's easy to be loyal when the going is easy. It's much harder to be loyal when the going gets rough. And yet, that's where it counts the most.

Loyalty to your partner is dependent on your level of loyalty to yourself. Do you live according to your innermost values? Are you loyal to what you believe in? Are you loyal to who you really are? Being loyal to someone else does not mean that you lose loyalty to your own being. That's not loyalty, it is lack of loyalty to Self.

Let's look at an example. You and your husband included in your wedding vows that you would live according to certain priorities, family and spiritual practices. Slowly, you notice that your husband's lifestyle demonstrates different priorities. The interminable hours that he spends at the office attest to the fact that his priority has become his work. Consequently, your children hardly know him, you are raising them without his support and your shared spiritual practices have dwindled to near extinction.

What should you do? What does being loyal mean for you?

Your first responsibility is always to yourself. If you are loyal to your Authentic Self, you know that this is not what you want to create. You know that this is not what your husband committed to doing and you know what the impact is on your children. Speak to your husband. Remind him of his commitment and his vow of loyalty to you and the children, and then make whatever decision you have to make to be loyal to yourself. Being loyal to yourself implies that you are following your own spiritual path. Sometimes being loyal to yourself means that you cannot be loyal to someone else. Follow what is true in your heart. In that, you can never go wrong.

If being loyal to yourself is in alignment with being loyal to your partner, you will benefit greatly both as individuals and as partners. Behind every great relationship are two loyal and powerful individuals.

Respect

Respect is defined in the Webster dictionary as "consider worthy of high regard." How do you consider your partner? Do you think positively of your partner? Do you take your partner for granted? Do you hold negative judgments about your partner? As mentioned earlier, we create a great team by focusing on its strength. The same is true for your partner. The more you hold your partner with high regard, the more you will start to see him or her that way and the more he or she will actually become that way.

We have witnessed this numerous times with our clients and friends. When one of the partners starts to criticize or point out negative traits about the other, the love dies a little in that person's heart. The opposite is also true. Try it yourself. For a whole day, think of your partner in the most flattering way possible. Think of how handsome or pretty he or she is. Think of how smart your partner is. Remind yourself of how generous and kind your partner is. Notice how you feel. Don't you feel great about your partner? The truth is your partner is probably a wonderful person most of the time. However, many partners focus on the negative traits. After a while, they are unable to see the positive aspects and they loose respect for their partner.

How do you hold your partner in your thoughts? Respect means holding your partner as worthy of high regard. Respect also means accepting and honoring differences. This is the hard part. Do you respect and honor your partner's idiosyncrasies? Do you honor and respect your partner's ideas and opinions, more specifically those that you don't agree with? Do you honor and respect the things your partner does that push your button?

Turn it around. Turn it within. Do you respect yourself? Are you ashamed of parts of yourself? Are you ashamed of some of your thoughts or emotions? Again, the outer reflects the inner. When you learn to respect yourself in all your "nooks and crannies;" when you learn to respect all your "gaucheries" and "platitudes" and when you learn to love all those parts of yourself for which you experience shame and embarrassment you will discover that respecting your partner comes much more easily.

Full of respect for each other, you can perceive the gift in the differences and learn to love what makes your partner so special. Another sure way to increase the synergy of your relationship!!!

YOUR SYNERGY CHECKLIST
REMEMBER:
You can increase your synergy on the path of spirit if you:
- Share a spiritual belief system and beliefs (understanding of God, metaphysics and religious dogmas)
- Share and practice spiritual practices together: prayer, meditation etc.
- Communicate openly and honestly about spiritual beliefs
- Take responsibility for your actions both individually and as a couple
- Take responsibility for your experience (your shadow parts) both individually and as a couple
- Are caring and compassionate towards each other
- Learn to forgive each other and yourself
- Give your partner acknowledgement on a constant basis
- Learn to acknowledge your mistakes and/or shortcomings without shame or guilt
- Are honest with yourself and your partner
- Are loyal with yourself and partner
- Respect yourself and your partner

How's your synergy doing?
In the next section, we discuss our journey on the path of the spirit

Danyelle Beaudry-Jones with Ron Jones

Our Journey on the Path of the Spirit

Our journey on the path of the spirit was the easiest one for us. We originally came together because of our spiritual beliefs and because of our commitment to our spiritual journey. However, as we ventured down the path of the spirit, we discovered that we had work to do in taking responsibility for our experience. The deeper we pushed each other's buttons, the harder this became for us. We also increased our ability to be honest with each other in acknowledging our mistakes and shortcomings.

The table that follows illustrates for each area of the spirit our initial level of synergy the level of synergy that we experienced when we first got together. It also shows how that initial level evolved after we did our individual and our couple's work. We again use the Synergy Continuum. You will recall, when we either "accept/honor" or "agree" with our partner's position, we create synergy. Of the two, agreement creates the greater synergy. When we "disagree with" or are "in contempt for" each other's position, on the other hand, we create separation in the relationship. Of those two, being in contempt creates the greater separation. You will notice that in more than half the areas on the path of the spirit we created synergy initially. This was because we had been on our spiritual path for a number of years and had been willing to do a great deal of our own inner healing work. We now discuss each one of these areas.

Areas of the Spirit	Synergy Level at the Beginning of Our Relationship	Synergy Level After We Did Our Healing Work
Spiritual beliefs	In agreement	In agreement
Spiritual practices	In disagreement	In agreement
Communication about spiritual beliefs	In agreement	In agreement

I'm Right...You Need to Change

Areas of the Spirit	Synergy Level at the Beginning of Our Relationship	Synergy Level After We Did Our Healing Work
Taking responsibility for our actions	In agreement	In agreement
Taking responsibility for our experience	In disagreement	In agreement
Caring and Compassionate attitude towards others and towards yourself	In agreement	In agreement
Forgiveness towards others and self	In contempt	In agreement
Giving others acknowledgment	In disagreement	In agreement
Acknowledging mistakes and shortcomings	In disagreement	In agreement
Honesty	In agreement	In agreement
Loyalty	In agreement	In agreement
Respect	In agreement	In agreement

Our Spiritual Beliefs

As mentioned, Ron and I shared common spiritual beliefs at the onset of our relationship. We both did a lot of work identifying what was true for us and what we choose to believe. We both believed that God was within and that God's nature was love and compassion.

We also believed that as human beings, we were co-creators of our destiny. In other words, we believed that by the choices we made in thoughts, emotions and deeds we had the power to create the life we wanted.

Our relationship to a higher presence in our life was empowering. These beliefs enabled us to experience a high level of synergy and to empower how we created our relationship on a daily basis.

Our Spiritual Practices

When we started sharing our life together, meditation and prayer was a daily practice in my life. I had understood through our communication via email before we got together that it was the same for Ron. However, it turned out that he wasn't ready to share those practices with me. I became very judgmental and angry, as this was one of my priority goals. The anger was identical to what I had experienced with my father when I wanted him to share the excitement I felt with the things I was passionate about as a child. Once again, I experienced disappointment and anger.

I shared those insights with Ron. After a few weeks of re-experiencing those childhood memories and reliving the anger in my body, I was able to disassociate my childhood wound from the present situation with Ron. I released my need for him to join me in daily practices. I accepted and embraced that his need was different from mine and that he had his own path to follow.

Letting go of my attachment to sharing my practices created the space for Ron to choose for himself. We started praying and meditating together shortly afterwards.

To this day, we pray and meditate together. Our choice is our own, and we give each other the leeway to freely engage in the practices that are in accordance with our individual paths. We moved from disagreement to agreement, and we achieved a high level of synergy based on mutual respect and acknowledgment of our inner individualized wisdom.

Communicating about Spiritual Beliefs

Sharing our spiritual beliefs and experiences has been an important source of joy for both of us since the beginning of our relationship. Understanding how the universe works, what metaphysical principles are and how they apply to our life is a passion we share. The satisfaction we experience together at discovering new insights continues to enrich our relationship.

Taking Responsibility for Our Actions

Ron and I trained ourselves years ago to recognize that we were responsible for our own actions. This was a belief and a practice that we shared when we first embarked on creating a successful relationship. Being able to recognize and to take responsibility for our own actions has enabled us to move quickly through issues and to make clear choices in our life.

Taking Responsibility for Our Experience (Our Shadow Parts)

Ron and I knew that how we experienced specific situations and incidents was contingent on our inner reality and our inner wounds. So on a conceptual level, we agreed. However, as with most couples, when we started working on our core issues, those that drive our life in a subconscious way, we found ourselves unable to separate our experience from what we saw in our partner.

Let's illustrate with a few examples. In certain instances, Ron would communicate information to me. This could be information related to incidents in the world or his thoughts about other people. I often asked questions to gain a deeper knowledge. Ron often reacted with anger and he would ask me why I couldn't simply listen to him. He would justify his anger by saying that if I really listened, I wouldn't need to ask questions. The fact was I was asking questions and he was getting angry. After several discussions around the fact that I was not responsible for his reaction to my questions, he started looking within and discovered that he interpreted my questions as a statement that he didn't know what he was talking about. He had a lot of anger at his parents for not listening to him as a child and had interpreted that as not being good enough. My asking questions brought him back to that core wound.

In another example, Ron would express anger and I would immediately get sad, convinced that my feeling of sadness was related to Ron's anger. In other words, I made him responsible for my sadness. It took me quite a while before I was able to discover the core wound hidden under that belief. As mentioned, I often experienced anger from my dad as a child. I craved his attention and his love and did not experience receiving it. Ron's anger brought me back to my childhood sadness at not receiving the love I wanted from my dad. I wasn't able to simply accept the reality of Ron's anger and to discern whether he was projecting it on me or not. I couldn't perceive his anger for what it was. I was immersed in my own sadness. It was only when I was able to re-experience those childhood memories and their inherent emotions that I was able to simply receive his expression of anger.

These two examples illustrate how important it was for us to do our inner healing work in order to expand our ability to be responsible for our own experience. Ron and I moved from disagreement to agreement and increased our ability to uncover who we really are as individuals and as couple.

Caring and Compassionate Attitude Towards Others and Towards Yourself

Ron and I have a lot of compassion for others and for ourselves. We have done enough work on ourselves to know that all human beings are the same and that another's shortcomings are only a reflection of our own. However, we did experience a lower level of compassion for each other when we were stuck in our own core wounds. For example, stuck in my own sadness, I had little compassion for Ron when he got angry. And stuck in his wound of not being good enough, Ron had little compassion for me when I asked questions. Our partners bring out the best in us, but they also reveal our deepest wounds. The more Ron and accept all of who we are the greater our ability to have compassion for each other.

Forgiveness Towards Others and Towards Ourselves

This was one of the most painful areas of our relationship for me. When Ron and I got together, he would hold on to resentment, sometimes for weeks. He was trying to heal his own issues. As mentioned, Ron had trouble asking for what he wanted. He didn't believe that he was good enough. Why should he deserve to get what he wanted? I can understand his process now. However, earlier when he started exhibiting resentment towards me, I was devastated. I remember the deep sadness and the pain in my body. If he loved me, I reasoned, how could he stay angry with me? Couldn't he see how all this affected me? I wanted to leave; it was so painful. I had contempt for his resentment.

I shared my experience with Ron and remembered that when I was young, my mother held on to some of the things I had done. She had resentment. I remembered wondering why my mother was angry at me and asking her why. I remembered hearing:, "If you loved me, you would remember what you did." I had forgotten. But my mother hadn't. As I remembered specific childhood incidents, I re-experienced the devastating sadness in my heart, the experience of powerlessness when I attempted to get my mother to love me. I remembered the thoughts "I must have done something really wrong" and that "if she really loved me, she would forgive me."

This took months for me to heal. Ron was doing his own healing work at the same time. Forgiveness is not an issue for us any more. We are able to move quickly through the different steps of forgiveness and can create love and compassion by learning from the situations that occasionally occur in our life.

Acknowledging Others

It has always been easy for me to give acknowledgement. This comes from the fact that I know how it feels not to get it and that I trained myself to give a great deal of acknowledgment to my children. Sometimes we do the opposite of what we experienced as children because we know what it feels like. I approached our relationship with the same determination to supply Ron with constant acknowledgement.

However, he didn't do the same for me. After a while, I started experiencing sadness at not receiving the same in kind. We started sharing our truth about the issue.

The truth for Ron was that he didn't give himself any acknowledgment so it was difficult for him to give it to others. This stemmed from his never being good enough as a child. That is, since he didn't experience receiving acknowledgment as a child, he never developed the habit of giving it.

As for me, it was an opportunity to heal the childhood wound around never receiving acknowledgment as a child. I had a deep inner longing to be recognized by my parents as a wonderful and loving human being. I was still holding on to the sadness of never having received that acknowledgment.

As you will note on the Synergy Continuum, we have moved from disagreement to agreement. We both recognize the benefit of giving each other acknowledgment. We know how nurturing that experience can be as it heals past wounds and builds up from within love and compassion. Every time we acknowledge each other, we are acknowledging ourselves. What we project on the other comes right back to us.

Acknowledging Our Mistakes and Shortcomings

As a child, I often watched adults around me make mistakes, but I never witnessed any of them acknowledging them. I remember how I judged them as vain and arrogant. I remember wanting my parents to apologize for being unfair or unloving. I also remember thinking how much I would respect them if they did.

When I had my own children, I decided that I would acknowledge my mistakes and apologize if I did anything that hurt them. When Ron and I got together, I maintained those behaviors. As a child, Ron had never observed adults acknowledging mistakes and shortcomings either. However, unlike me, he had had no judgments about such behaviors. Therefore, he modeled his own behaviors on what he had observed and not on his judgments of those observations. It wasn't easy for him to acknowledge his mistakes and shortcomings.

After a while, I started feeling anger at the fact that he wouldn't acknowledge his mistakes and shortcomings. I was willing to do it and wanted him to do it too. I had discovered on my spiritual path that the Ego hates to admit when a mistake is made. The Ego wants to be right and strives to save face instead of acknowledging the truth.

Admitting mistakes puts the Higher Self in charge of the Ego. On the spiritual path it is essential to acknowledge one's mistakes and shortcomings. Ron and I talked about this area of our relationship. He watched me do it and noticed that he had a belief that he would die if he acknowledged his mistakes and his shortcomings. In fact, his Ego was afraid to die. He started practicing acknowledging his mistakes and shortcomings and observed not only that he survived but also that it increased the synergy in our relationship. The truth about a situation always creates synergy in a relationship.

Honesty, Loyalty and Respect

Our commitment to our spiritual path and to each other has driven our behaviors. We are honest because we chose to be. When we did avoid mentioning certain things a few times, our commitment was such that we admitted our reluctance and shared the information.

We are loyal to ourselves first. We are committed to speaking our truth and to living our life according to the principles we believe in. We share similar beliefs. Being loyal to ourselves and to each other is easy. Ron and I have a lot of respect for each other. We both believe that we are doing the best that we can. We trust that our partner is honest and that he/she will follow-through on commitments. Honesty, loyalty and respect have contributed to deepening our relationship and have enabled us to navigate through troubled waters. These qualities have been our anchors on our journey on the path of spirit.

We have completed the journey on the five paths of synergy for couples. Let's take a look at how these five paths work together to further increase the synergy of your relationship.

Chapter 9

Working the Five Paths Together

Each of the five paths is different in nature and requires specific tools and abilities. You don't learn to express emotions responsibly in the same way that you learn to manage a budget. In order to create synergy in your relationship, you and your partner must travel down the five paths at one time or another. At this point, you may want to focus on a specific area on the path of the will. For example, you may be struggling with your commitment to the relationship, or the issues that you are facing at this time may be more emotional. You and your partner may have trouble expressing anger together or you may be afraid to reveal the shame you are carrying as a result of childhood trauma. These issues are on the path of the heart. Eventually, you may also need to hold a vision together for your future or to successfully manage your budget together. Some time down the road you will have to do some form of healing work on all five paths.

An intimate relationship engages all of who we are. As human beings, we have a mind, a heart, a body, a will and a spirit. We relate to others in all of these dimensions and we create synergy or separation in these same dimensions. As emphasized throughout, creating a successful relationship requires that you consciously choose to increase your level of synergy in all the dimensions of your relationship.

To start improving your level of synergy, you must identify the areas that require improvement. Take the time to identify the issue that drains your level of synergy. What creates separation in your relationship at this time? What issues show up on a weekly basis? Is it managing your finances? Do you have trouble agreeing on priorities for balancing your budget? Are you experiencing difficulties in saving money? Maybe your issues are related to sharing a common vision and similar goals? Is the way you raise your children the issue? Or is it sharing common spiritual practices? Focus on the key issue and find the tools that you need to work it through.

As you work through the key issue, you will discover that you also need to focus on at least one other path. For example, your key issue may be managing your finances together. You don't agree on how to save money and you have endless discussions on that subject. As you start working through this issue, you notice that you also need to learn to differentiate between facts and judgments. How do you spend money? What are the facts? What are your judgments on how you spend money or how your partner spends money?

Managing money is an area on the path of the body. Differentiating between facts and judgments is an area on the path of the mind. In this instance, both paths are working together to enable you to increase the financial synergy in your relationship. You may also discover that you are experiencing a great deal of anger towards your partner in relation to how he or she spends money. You may experience difficulty in communicating that anger in a responsible way. Expressing anger responsibly is an area on the path of the heart. You now have three paths working together.

In short, while the issue at hand, managing money, is on the path of the body, to work through your issue also requires the use of the tool "fact, judgment and emotion," which is on the path of the mind. Finally, you also have to learn to express anger in a responsible way, one of the areas on the path of the heart.

All five paths can potentially work together depending on the issue you are working on. The challenge for all couples is to develop the ability to discern the key issue and then link it to other areas from other paths. The key issue is the prevalent symptom of separation in your relationship. It is the subject of conflict, the recurring problem that keeps showing up again and again.

Over a period of a week, notice what you fight about. Identify your key issue.

Take the time to define it clearly. What are you fighting about? What facts and judgments do you have about that key issue? Practice communicating about the situation and learn to speak about it in a structured and precise way. What emotions are you feeling? Share your emotions with your partner. Listen to your partner's emotions.

I'm Right...You Need to Change

To find a solution, list your needs, those of your partner and those of the relationship. As we mentioned earlier, your relationship is a third entity that has specific needs. Couples who have created successful relationships recognize this and manage their conflicts and make decisions accordingly.

Let's use the example of managing your finances.

Key Issue: You want to save 10 percent of your combined income in a retirement plan. Your partner always comes up with new expenses for the house or for entertainment purposes.

Facts: You decide to list the facts around this issue. Your partner does the same. You share your lists and come up with a combined list of facts. For example: You have no savings plan. You have saved 1 percent of your income over a period of a year. You exceed your budget by 8 percent every year.

Judgments: You have judgments about your partner. You think that your partner is irresponsible. Your partner also has judgments about you. Your partner finds you too controlling.

You share those judgments.

Emotions: You feel a lot of anger towards your partner. Your partner also has a lot of anger towards you. You share those emotions responsibly, allowing for the full expression of the emotional charge. You both take responsibility for your emotions and refrain from blaming each other. You now have a complete understanding of the situation.

You are ready to find a solution.

Needs and Wants: You write down your needs and wants. For example: You need to have a retirement plan. You want to retire at 50 years of age and you maintain your present standard of living.

Your partner writes down his/her needs. For example: Your partner needs to exercise regularly. You partner needs to have at least two weeks of vacation a year. Your partner wants to attend musical concerts at least five times a year.

Together, write the needs of your relationship. For example: Your relationship needs for both of you to come up with a plan fully supported by both partners. Your relationship needs to establish a plan for the future. Your relationship needs to fulfill all of the partner's individual needs.

Action Plan: Together, you start listing the possible actions that you can take. You identify the specific amounts required to satisfy your partner's needs. Are there more economical ways to achieve the same goals? Maybe your partner can attend the YMCA instead of purchasing a membership at a country club.

You identify what income is left after you have fulfilled all of your living requirements. You come up with an amount that you can dedicate to your retirement fund. You finalize the list of actions that you can take to meet all of your needs yours, your partner's, and those of your relationship. Have all of your needs been met? Revisit your action plan and revise it until all of your needs are met.

As individuals we are constantly learning, growing and discovering new aspects of our Self. You are not the same person at 30, 40 or 50 that you were at 20. Your partner also continues to evolve and to reveal new parts of him or herself. Just as human beings constantly adjust to new discoveries about themselves, your relationship continues to evolve by adjusting to the individual transformations that occur within you.

This is a normal evolutionary process. Change is normal. Stability is not. If you are striving to "fix" your relationship once and for all, if you are looking to solve all of your problems and prevent new ones from occurring, or if you are looking for the perfect and stable relationship, you will only succeed in destroying the fundamental essence of your relationship.

A relationship is a living and evolving organization. It needs to remain flexible. It is constantly transforming itself. To successfully manage your relationship, focus on learning tools, such as those presented here, that will enable you to manage change. Don't focus on finding the "perfect" and "final" solution to your problems of the past and the potential issues of the future. Dedicate yourself to increasing your abilities and skills in the five paths. For example, learn to express your emotions responsibly on the path of the heart. Develop the ability to discern facts from judgments on the path of the mind. Practice optimistic self-talk on the path of the will. Learn to source yourself from within on the path of the spirit. Develop skills to effectively manage your physical resources on the path of the body.

The better you learn to use the tools of the five paths, the more proficient you become at using them on a daily basis. Your chances at creating a loving and energizing relationship with your partner will increase in proportion to your increased level of ability and skill. Together you will be able to constantly create your relationship anew. Courage and determination will replace fear and paralysis. Your level of joy and love will continue to grow, and you will experience a level of synergy beyond your greatest expectations.

The glorious joy of being in a couple

I love being with you,
I love sharing my most intimate feelings with you,
I love how you hold me and gently stroke my body,
I love how we dream together of building a home, of going on a trip or of simply going to the movies
I love how you cry in my arms and give me the treasures of your heart.
I love how you kick my butt when I need it and support me to be the best that I can be
Alone I am strong with you I am invincible
Alone I am happy with you I shower my joy in the world
Alone I can live a great life with you I dream of a greater life for others
Your love for me is the key that opens my heart to others
My mind loves to play with your mind, my heart cherishes your heart, my body desires your body, my spirit honors your spirit
I am so grateful for all of you, I am so grateful for the deep synergy of our minds, hearts, bodies, wills and spirits.

Danyelle Beaudry-Jones, 2001

How to get in touch with the authors.

Ron and Danyelle Jones are co-founders of Voel Inc. an organization dedicated to "transforming world consciousness one person at a time."

They conduct workshops, couples' retreats and classes and lead individual and couples' coaching sessions.

They also travel throughout the United States and Canada for speaking engagements. They live in Kansas City, Kansas and in Montreal, Canada.

You can reach them at voelinc@voelinc.com.

To find out about their upcoming events, visit their website at www.voelinc.com

How to order I'm Right ... You Need to Change

You can order this book directly from AuthorHouse at www.authorhouse.com or by calling their book order hotline at 1-888-280-7715.